Van and RV Camping in State Forests

Discover 585 Camping Areas at 298 Forests in 25 States

Van and RV Camping in State Forests, copyright © 2023 by Ted Houghton. Printed and bound in the United States of America. All rights reserved. No part of this publication may be reproduced in any form without the prior written permission from the publisher.

Although efforts are made to ensure the accuracy of this publication, the author and Roundabout Publications shall have neither liability nor responsibility to any person or entity with respect to any loss or damage caused, or alleged to be caused, directly or indirectly by the information contained in this publication.

Published by:

Roundabout Publications
PO Box 569
LaCygne, KS 66040

Phone: 800-455-2207
Internet: www.RoundaboutPublications.com

Library of Congress Control Number: 2023937503

ISBN-10: 1-885464-89-4
ISBN-13: 978-1-885464-89-7

Table of Contents

Alabama	5
California	7
Connecticut	10
Florida	12
Illinois	17
Indiana	19
Iowa	22
Louisiana	24
Maryland	26
Massachusetts	28
Michigan	31
Minnesota	42
Missouri	48
Montana	50
New Hampshire	52
New Jersey	54
New York	56
North Dakota	62
Ohio	64
Oregon	66
Pennsylvania	69
Tennessee	71
Washington	73
West Virginia	78
Wisconsin	80

Introduction

Huge portions of public lands, managed by a variety of government agencies, are available to the general public for recreational use. This book will guide you to 585 camping areas available from various State Agencies in 25 states.

You can learn more about these camping locations by visiting a state's department of natural resources, parks and/or tourism website. Please note that sites with tent camping only and areas accessible only by boat are not included in this guide.

Using This Guide

The guide is especially helpful when used along with Google Maps, Windows Maps, or a GPS device for locating and navigating to each camping area.

State Maps

A state map is provided to aid you in locating the camping areas. A grid overlay on each map is used when cross-referencing with each camping area.

Map Grid Chart & Alphabetical List

Following the state map is a chart showing the camping area ID number(s) located within a map grid. Following this chart is an alphabetical list of each camping area, which is especially helpful when you already know the name of an area. This list provides each location's ID number and map grid location.

Camping Area Details

Camping area details include information about each public camping area within the state. Preceding each location's name is the ID number and map grid location, which is used when referencing the state map.

Details for each camping area generally include the following information:

- Total number of sites or dispersed camping
- Number of RV sites
- Sites with electric hookups
- Full hookup sites, if available
- Water (central location or spigots at site)
- Showers
- RV dump station
- Toilets (flush, pit/vault, or none)
- Laundry facilities
- Camp store
- Maximum RV size limits (if any)
- Reservation information (accepted, not accepted, recommended or required)
- Generator use and hours (if limited)
- Operating season
- Camping fees charged
- Miscellaneous notes
- Length of stay limit
- Elevation in feet and meters
- Telephone number
- Nearby city or town
- GPS coordinates

The Ultimate Public Campground Project

Data for this publication is from The Ultimate Public Campground Project, which was established in 2008 to provide a consolidated and comprehensive source for public campgrounds of all types. Please note that despite our best efforts, there will always be errors to be found in the data. With over 45,000 records in our database, it is impossible to ensure that each one is always up-to-date.

Update: In 2022 The Ultimate Public Campground Project database was acquired by a GPS manufacturer. As a result, updated information for this book will no longer be available - this is the last edition.

Happy Camping!

Common Abbreviations Used

CG	Campground
CR	County Road
MP	Milepost
TC	Trail Camp
TH	Trail head

Area Designations

DSF	Demonstration State Forest
RA	Recreation Area
SF	State Forest
WA	Wildlife Area

Miscellaneous Agencies

DEC	Department of Conservation
DNR	Department of Natural Resources
DNRC	Department of Natural Resources & Conservation
KRMB	Kickapoo Reserve Management Board
MDC	Missouri Department of Conservation

Alabama

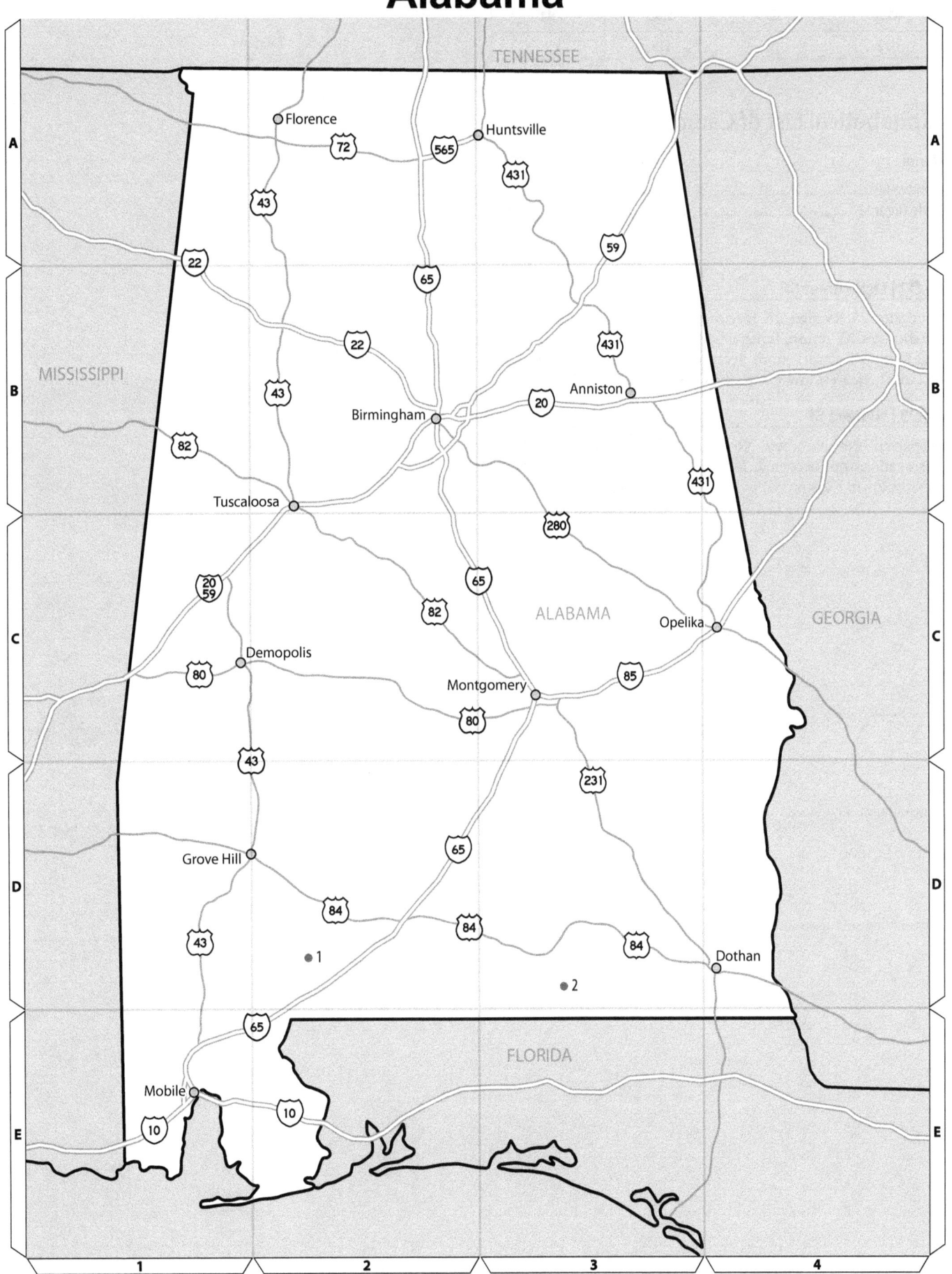

Map	ID	Map	ID
D2	1	D3	2

Alphabetical List of Camping Areas

Name	ID	Map
Geneva SF	2	D3
Little River SF	1	D2

1 • D2 | Little River SF

Total sites: 25, RV sites: 15, Elec sites: 15, Water at site, Flush toilet, No showers, RV dump, Tents: $15/RVs: $25-30, Also cabins, Some Full hookups, Reservations accepted, Elev: 198ft/60m, Tel: 251-862-2022, Nearest town: Atmore. GPS: 31.256818, -87.482169

2 • D3 | Geneva SF

Dispersed sites, No water, No toilets, Tent & RV camping: Free, Reservations not accepted, Elev: 226ft/69m, Tel: 334-898-7013, Nearest town: Kinston. GPS: 31.142836, -86.184736

California

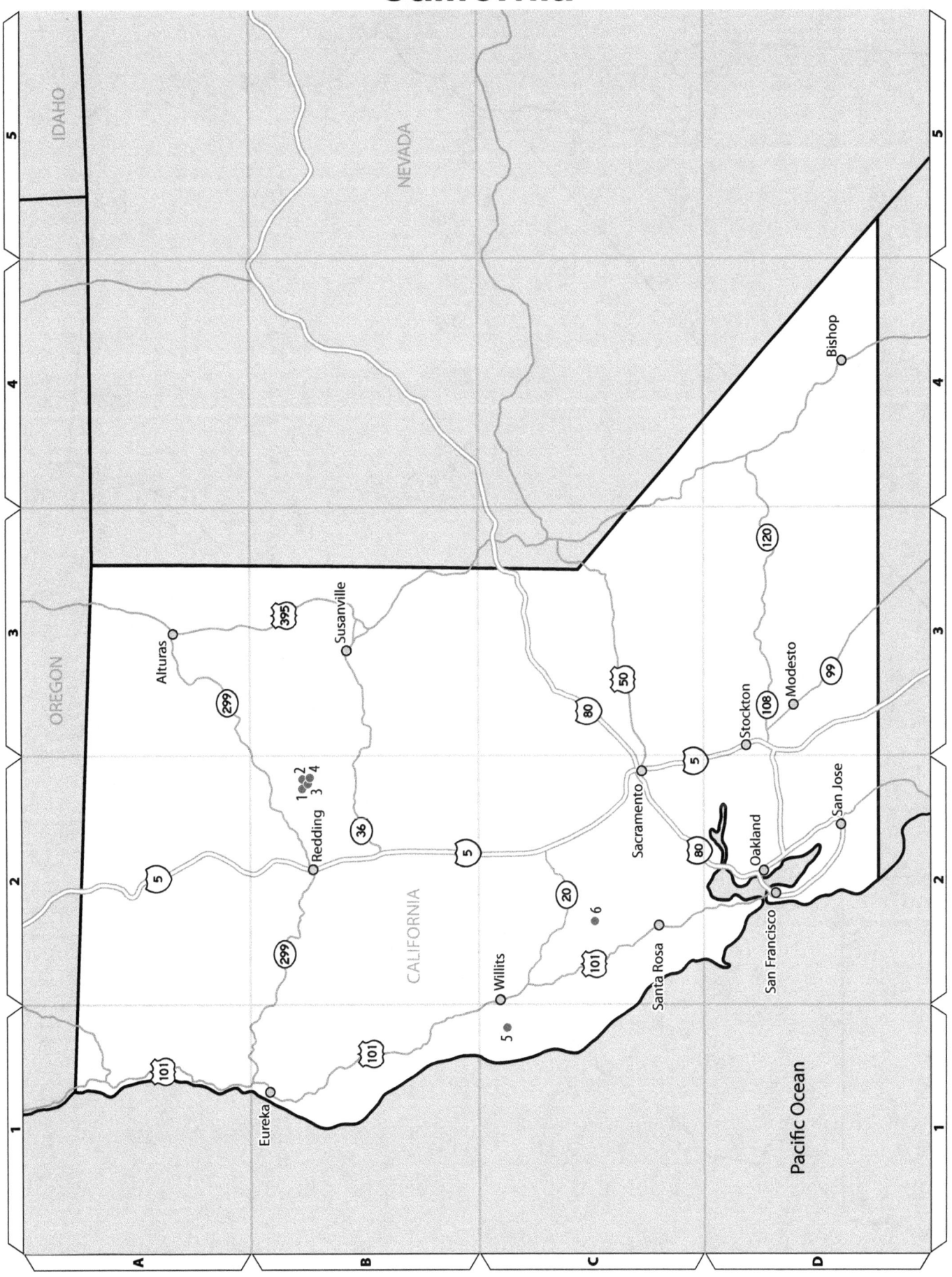

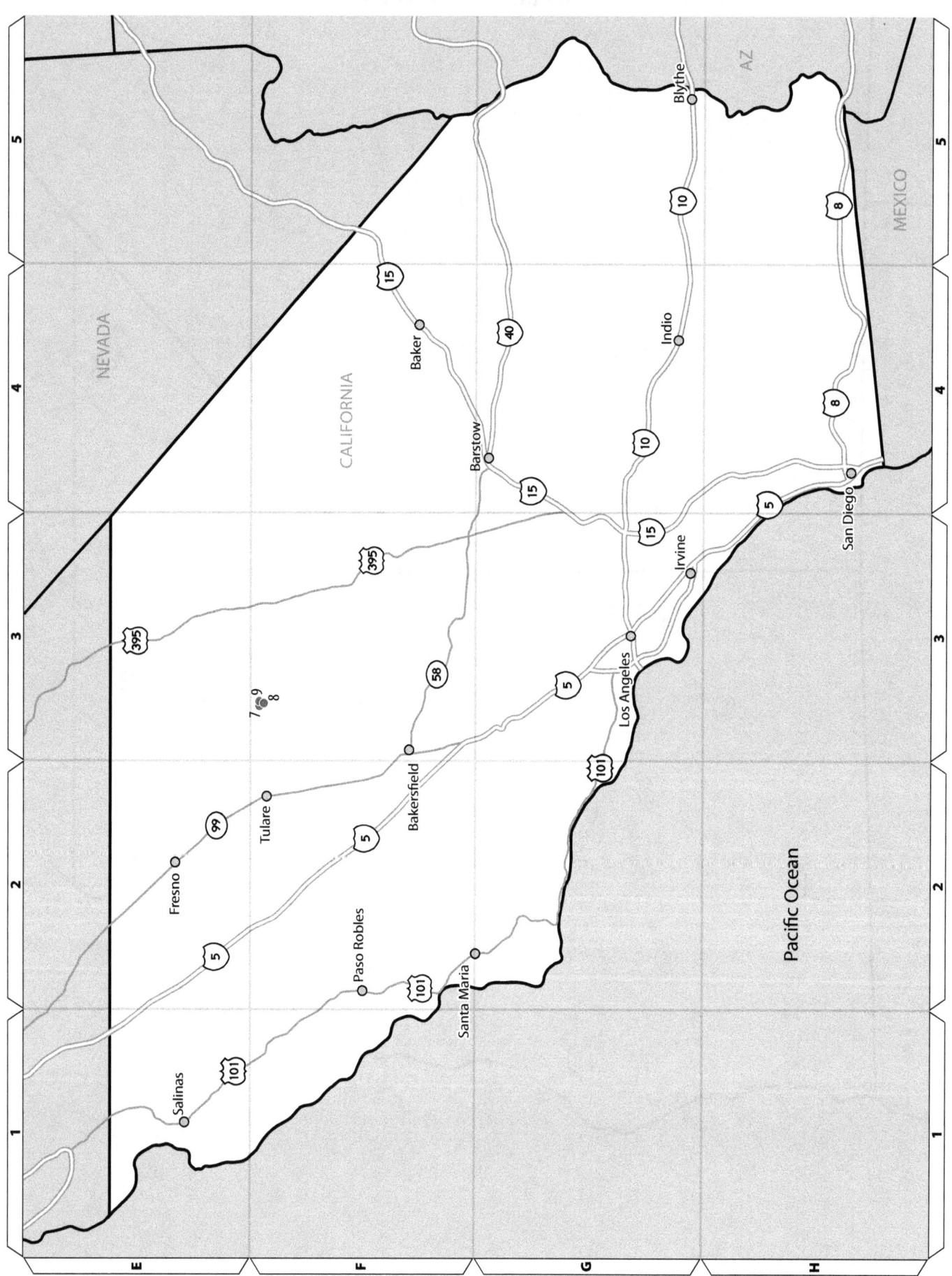

Map	ID	Map	ID
B2	1-4	C2	6
C1	5	F3	7-9

Alphabetical List of Camping Areas

Name	ID	Map
Boggs Mountain SF - Calso Camp	6	C2
Jackson SF - Horse Camp	5	C1
Latour DSF - Butcher Gulch	1	B2
Latour DSF - Old Cow Creek	2	B2
Latour DSF - Old Station	3	B2
Latour DSF - South Cow Creek	4	B2
Mountain Home SF - Frazier Mill	7	F3
Mountain Home SF - Hedrick Pond	8	F3
Mountain Home SF - Shake Camp	9	F3

1 • B2 | Latour DSF - Butcher Gulch

Dispersed sites, Central water, Vault/pit toilet, No showers, No RV dump, Tent & RV camping: Free, Open Jun-Oct, Reservations not accepted, Elev: 5177ft/1578m, Tel: 530-225-2438, Nearest town: Redding. GPS: 40.665692, -121.739556

2 • B2 | Latour DSF - Old Cow Creek

Total sites: 3, RV sites: 3, Central water, Vault/pit toilet, No showers, No RV dump, Tent & RV camping: Free, Open Jun-Oct, Max Length: 25ft, Reservations not accepted, Elev: 5837ft/1779m, Tel: 530-225-2438, Nearest town: Redding. GPS: 40.661724, -121.676145

3 • B2 | Latour DSF - Old Station

Dispersed sites, Central water, Vault/pit toilet, No showers, No RV dump, Tent & RV camping: Free, Open Jun-Oct, Reservations not accepted, Elev: 5786ft/1764m, Tel: 530-225-2438, Nearest town: Redding. GPS: 40.641047, -121.694608

4 • B2 | Latour DSF - South Cow Creek

Total sites: 4, RV sites: 4, Central water, Vault/pit toilet, No showers, No RV dump, Tent & RV camping: Free, Open Jun-Oct, Max Length: 30ft, Reservations not accepted, Elev: 5647ft/1721m, Tel: 530-225-2438, Nearest town: Redding. GPS: 40.627738, -121.677813

5 • C1 | Jackson SF - Horse Camp

Total sites: 8, No water, Vault/pit toilet, Tent & RV camping: $15, Elev: 517ft/158m, Tel: 707-964-5674, Nearest town: Fort Bragg. GPS: 39.346949, -123.540329

6 • C2 | Boggs Mountain SF - Calso Camp

Total sites: 14, RV sites: 14, No water, Vault/pit toilet, Tent & RV camping: $10, Elev: 3271ft/997m, Tel: 707-928-4378, Nearest town: Cobb. GPS: 38.829775, -122.698184

7 • F3 | Mountain Home SF - Frazier Mill

Total sites: 49, RV sites: 49, Central water, Vault/pit toilet, No showers, No RV dump, Tent & RV camping: $15, Open May-Oct, Max Length: 21ft, Reservations not accepted, Elev: 6362ft/1939m, Tel: 559-539-2321, Nearest town: Springville. GPS: 36.237236, -118.689566

8 • F3 | Mountain Home SF - Hedrick Pond

Total sites: 14, RV sites: 5, Central water, Vault/pit toilet, No showers, No RV dump, Tent & RV camping: $15, Open May-Oct, Max Length: 20ft, Reservations not accepted, Elev: 6368ft/1941m, Tel: 559-539-2321, Nearest town: Springville. GPS: 36.229668, -118.680647

9 • F3 | Mountain Home SF - Shake Camp

Total sites: 15, RV sites: 15, Central water, Vault/pit toilet, No showers, No RV dump, Tent & RV camping: $15, No large RVs, Open May-Oct, Max Length: 20ft, Reservations not accepted, Elev: 6562ft/2000m, Tel: 559-539-2321, Nearest town: Springville. GPS: 36.249242, -118.671054

Connecticut

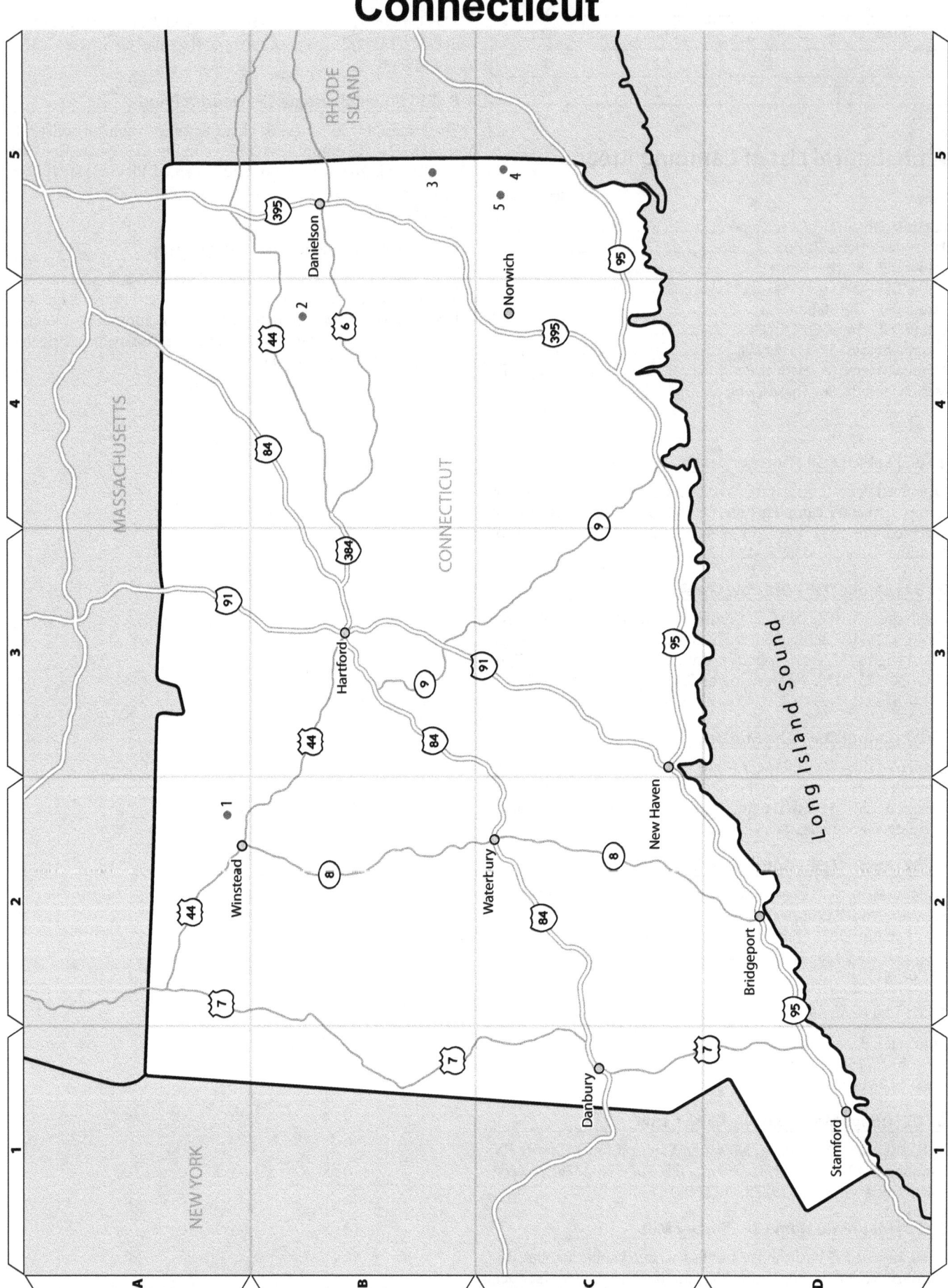

Map	ID	Map	ID
A2	1	B5	3
B4	2	C5	4-5

Alphabetical List of Camping Areas

Name	ID	Map
American Legion SF - Austin F. Hawes	1	A2
Natchaug SF - Silvermine Horse Camp	2	B4
Pachaug SF - Frog Hollow Horse Camp	3	B5
Pachaug SF - Green Falls	4	C5
Pachaug SF - Mount Misery	5	C5

1 • A2 | American Legion SF - Austin F. Hawes

Total sites: 30, RV sites: 30, Central water, Flush toilet, Free showers, RV dump, Tent & RV camping: $27, CT residents: $17, Stay limit: 14 days, Open Apr-Oct, Max Length: 35ft, Reservations accepted, Elev: 489ft/149m, Tel: 860-379-0922, Nearest town: Pleasant Valley. GPS: 41.935409, -73.002787

2 • B4 | Natchaug SF - Silvermine Horse Camp

Total sites: 15, RV sites: 15, No water, Vault/pit toilet, Tent & RV camping: Free, Open Apr-Nov, Reservations not accepted, Elev: 732ft/223m, Tel: 860-974-1562, Nearest town: Eastford. GPS: 41.827525, -72.079862

3 • B5 | Pachaug SF - Frog Hollow Horse Camp

Total sites: 18, RV sites: 18, No water, Vault/pit toilet, Tents: Free/RVs: $24, Open Apr-Nov, Reservations not accepted, Elev: 367ft/112m, Tel: 860-376-4075, Nearest town: Voluntown. GPS: 41.638154, -71.814303

4 • C5 | Pachaug SF - Green Falls

Total sites: 18, RV sites: 18, No water, Vault/pit toilet, Tent & RV camping: $27, CT residents: $14, Open Apr-Sep, Elev: 381ft/116m, Tel: 860-376-4075, Nearest town: Voluntown. GPS: 41.536793, -71.809985

5 • C5 | Pachaug SF - Mount Misery

Total sites: 22, RV sites: 22, Central water, Vault/pit toilet, No showers, No RV dump, Tent & RV camping: $24, CT residents: $14, Open Apr-Dec, Elev: 256ft/78m, Tel: 860-376-4075, Nearest town: Voluntown. GPS: 41.541437, -71.858387

Florida

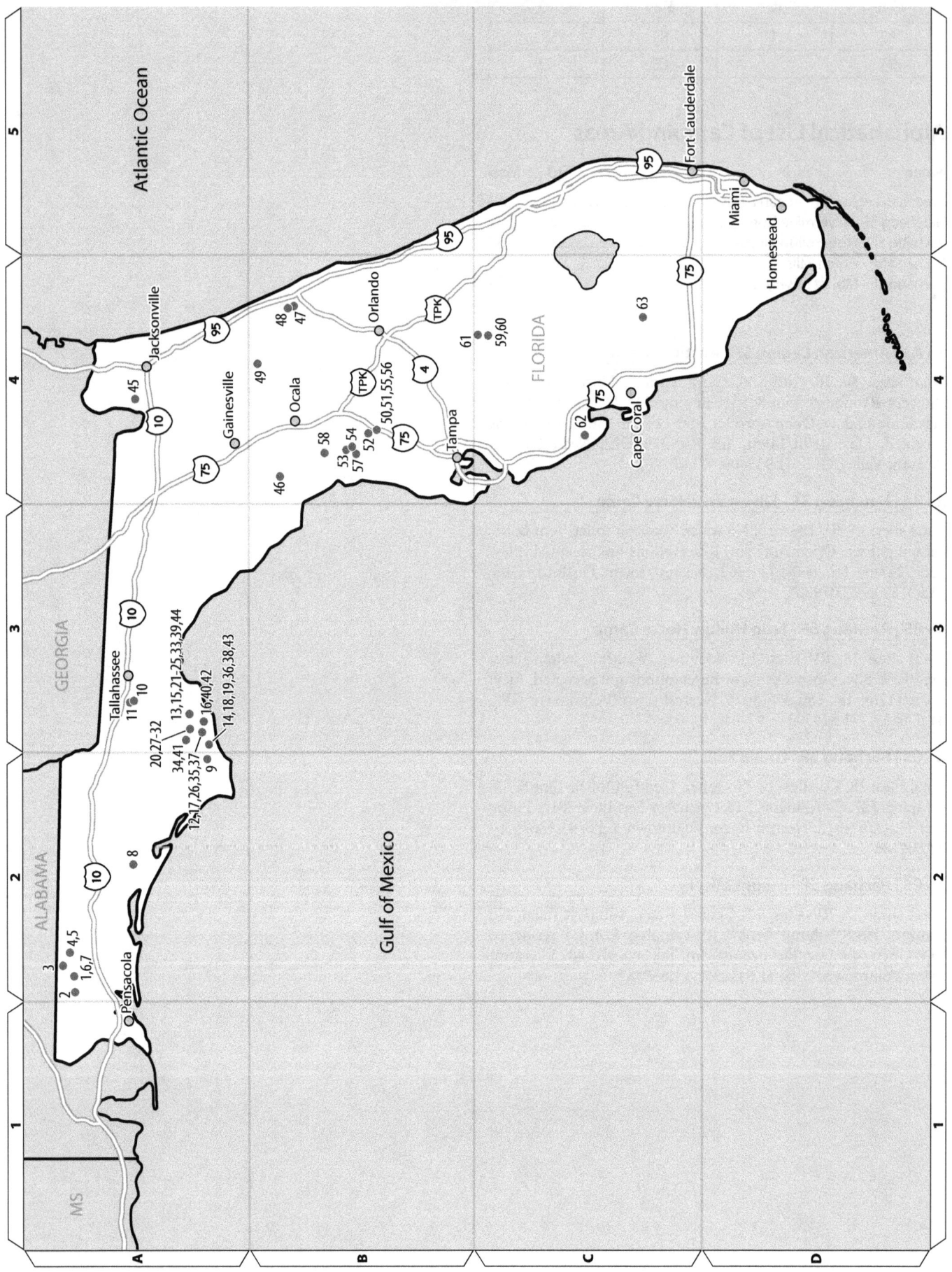

Map	ID	Map	ID
A2	1-9	B4	46-58
A3	10-44	C4	59-63
A4	45		

Alphabetical List of Camping Areas

Name	ID	Map
Blackwater River SF - Bear Lake	1	A2
Blackwater River SF - Coldwater Equestrian	2	A2
Blackwater River SF - Hurricane Lake North	3	A2
Blackwater River SF - Karick Lake North	4	A2
Blackwater River SF - Karick Lake South	5	A2
Blackwater River SF - Krul Area 1	6	A2
Blackwater River SF - Krul Area 2	7	A2
Cary SF	45	A4
Goethe SF - Black Prong	46	B4
Lake Talquin SF - Fort Braden Trailhead	10	A3
Lake Talquin SF - High Bluff	11	A3
Lake Wales Ridge SF - Reedy Creek	59	C4
Lakes Wales Ridge SF - Reedy Creek II Hunt Cmp	60	C4
Lakes Wales Ridge SF - Walk-in-the-Water	61	C4
Myakka SF - Flying A	62	C4
Okaloacoochie Slough SF - Wild Cow	63	C4
Pine Log SF - Sand Pond	8	A2
Tate's Hell SF - Borrow Pit	12	A3
Tate's Hell SF - Bus Stop	13	A3
Tate's Hell SF - Cash Creek	14	A3
Tate's Hell SF - Countyline OHV	15	A3
Tate's Hell SF - Crooked River #1	16	A3
Tate's Hell SF - Deep Creek	9	A2
Tate's Hell SF - Dew Drop	17	A3
Tate's Hell SF - Doyle Creek	18	A3
Tate's Hell SF - Dry Bridge	19	A3
Tate's Hell SF - Gully Branch	20	A3
Tate's Hell SF - Log Cabin #1	21	A3
Tate's Hell SF - Log Cabin #2	22	A3
Tate's Hell SF - Log Cabin #3	23	A3
Tate's Hell SF - Log Cabin #4	24	A3
Tate's Hell SF - Loop Road	25	A3
Tate's Hell SF - New River	26	A3
Tate's Hell SF - New River Camp #2	27	A3
Tate's Hell SF - New River Camp #3	28	A3
Tate's Hell SF - New River Camp #4	29	A3
Tate's Hell SF - New River Camp #5	30	A3
Tate's Hell SF - New River Camp #6	31	A3
Tate's Hell SF - New River Camp #7	32	A3
Tate's Hell SF - Nick's Road	33	A3
Tate's Hell SF - North Road Camp	34	A3
Tate's Hell SF - Parker Place	35	A3
Tate's Hell SF - Pidcock Road	36	A3
Tate's Hell SF - Pope Place	37	A3
Tate's Hell SF - Rake Creek	38	A3
Tate's Hell SF - Rock Landing	39	A3
Tate's Hell SF - Sunday Rollaway	40	A3
Tate's Hell SF - Unnamed	41	A3
Tate's Hell SF - Warren Bluff	42	A3
Tate's Hell SF - Whiskey George	43	A3
Tate's Hell SF - Womack Creek	44	A3
Tiger Bay SF - Bennett Field	47	B4
Tiger Bay SF - Tram Road Equestrian	48	B4
Welaka SF - Arabian Rd Equestrian Camp	49	B4
Withlacoochee SF - Croom Motorcycle RA - Buttgenbach	50	B4
Withlacoochee SF - Cypress Glen	51	B4
Withlacoochee SF - Hog Island	52	B4
Withlacoochee SF - Holder Mine RA	53	B4
Withlacoochee SF - Mutual Mine RA	54	B4
Withlacoochee SF - River Jct	55	B4
Withlacoochee SF - Silver Lake CG	56	B4
Withlacoochee SF - Tillis Hill Equestrian Camp	57	B4
Withlacoochee SF - Two Mile Prairie - Bear Head Hammock	58	B4

1 • A2 | Blackwater River SF - Bear Lake

Total sites: 40, RV sites: 32, Elec sites: 32, Water available, Flush toilet, Free showers, No RV dump, Tents: $9-14/RVs: $14, Stay limit: 14 days, Open all year, Max Length: 93ft, Reservations accepted, Elev: 141ft/43m, Tel: 850-983-5363, Nearest town: Munson. GPS: 30.861828, -86.834191

2 • A2 | Blackwater River SF - Coldwater Equestrian

Total sites: 56, RV sites: 55, Elec sites: 55, Water at site, Flush toilet, Free showers, Tents: $9-23/RVs: $14, Stay limit: 14 days, Open all year, Max Length: 60ft, Reservations required, Elev: 121ft/37m, Tel: 850-983-5363, Nearest town: Milton. GPS: 30.846889, -86.981891

3 • A2 | Blackwater River SF - Hurricane Lake North

Total sites: 18, RV sites: 13, Elec sites: 13, Water at site, Flush toilet, Free showers, No RV dump, Tent & RV camping: $14-24, Stay limit: 14 days, Open all year, Max Length: 57ft, Reservations accepted, Elev: 200ft/61m, Tel: 850-983-5363, Nearest town: Crestview. GPS: 30.944284, -86.754503

4 • A2 | Blackwater River SF - Karick Lake North

Total sites: 15, RV sites: 15, Elec sites: 15, Water available, Flush toilet, Free showers, Tent & RV camping: $14-24, Stay limit: 14 days, Open all year, Max Length: 60ft, Reservations accepted, Elev: 197ft/60m, Tel: 850-957-5700, Nearest town: Baker. GPS: 30.895909, -86.641434

5 • A2 | Blackwater River SF - Karick Lake South

Total sites: 15, RV sites: 15, Elec sites: 15, Water available, Flush toilet, Free showers, No RV dump, Tent & RV camping: $14-24, Stay limit: 14 days, Open all year, Max Length: 55ft, Reservations accepted, Elev: 151ft/46m, Tel: 850-983-5363, Nearest town: Baker. GPS: 30.893911, -86.644451

6 • A2 | Blackwater River SF - Krul Area 1

Total sites: 22, RV sites: 17, Elec sites: 17, Water at site, Flush toilet, Free showers, No RV dump, Tent & RV camping: $14, No pets, Stay limit: 14 days, Open all year, Max Length: 58ft, Elev: 141ft/43m, Tel: 850-983-5363, Nearest town: Munson. GPS: 30.862072, -86.852175

7 • A2 | Blackwater River SF - Krul Area 2

Total sites: 28, RV sites: 28, Elec sites: 28, Water at site, Flush toilet, Free showers, No RV dump, Tent & RV camping: $14, No pets, Stay limit: 14 days, Open all year, Max Length: 73ft, Elev: 107ft/33m, Tel: 850-983-5363, Nearest town: Munson. GPS: 30.862687, -86.850387

8 • A2 | Pine Log SF - Sand Pond

Total sites: 20, RV sites: 20, Elec sites: 20, Water at site, Flush toilet, Free showers, RV dump, Tent & RV camping: $24, Open all year, Elev: 102ft/31m, Tel: 850-535-2888, Nearest town: Ebro. GPS: 30.429196, -85.881619

9 • A2 | Tate's Hell SF - Deep Creek

Dispersed sites, No toilets, Tent & RV camping: $10, Stay limit: 14 days, Open all year, Reservations not accepted, Elev: 20ft/6m, Tel: 850-697-3734, Nearest town: Carrabelle. GPS: 29.859266, -84.967512

10 • A3 | Lake Talquin SF - Fort Braden Trailhead

Dispersed sites, No water, Vault/pit toilet, Tent & RV camping: $10, Elev: 184ft/56m, Tel: 850-488-1871, Nearest town: Tallahassee. GPS: 30.439629, -84.495406

11 • A3 | Lake Talquin SF - High Bluff

Total sites: 32, RV sites: 30, No water, Vault/pit toilet, Tent & RV camping: $10, Stay limit: 14 days, Open all year, Max Length: 16ft, Reservations accepted, Elev: 128ft/39m, Tel: 850-681-5950, Nearest town: Tallahassee. GPS: 30.459842, -84.498446

12 • A3 | Tate's Hell SF - Borrow Pit

Dispersed sites, No water, Vault/pit toilet, Tent & RV camping: $10, Stay limit: 14 days, Open all year, Reservations not accepted, Elev: 13ft/4m, Tel: 850-697-3734, Nearest town: Carrabelle. GPS: 29.916789, -84.735421

13 • A3 | Tate's Hell SF - Bus Stop

Dispersed sites, No water, Vault/pit toilet, Tent & RV camping: $10, Stay limit: 14 days, Open all year, Reservations not accepted, Elev: 30ft/9m, Tel: 850-697-3734, Nearest town: Carrabelle. GPS: 29.981089, -84.625925

14 • A3 | Tate's Hell SF - Cash Creek

Dispersed sites, No toilets, Tent & RV camping: $10, Stay limit: 14 days, Open all year, Reservations not accepted, Elev: 7ft/2m, Tel: 850-697-3734, Nearest town: Carrabelle. GPS: 29.816381, -84.836876

15 • A3 | Tate's Hell SF - Countyline OHV

Dispersed sites, No toilets, Tent & RV camping: $10, Stay limit: 14 days, Open all year, Reservations not accepted, Elev: 30ft/9m, Tel: 850-697-3734, Nearest town: Carrabelle. GPS: 30.010907, -84.617989

16 • A3 | Tate's Hell SF - Crooked River #1

Dispersed sites, No water, Vault/pit toilet, Tent & RV camping: $10, Stay limit: 14 days, Open all year, Reservations not accepted, Elev: 5ft/2m, Tel: 850-697-3734, Nearest town: Carrabelle. GPS: 29.908738, -84.601833

17 • A3 | Tate's Hell SF - Dew Drop

Dispersed sites, No water, Vault/pit toilet, Tent & RV camping: $10, Stay limit: 14 days, Open all year, Reservations not accepted, Elev: 30ft/9m, Tel: 850-697-3734, Nearest town: Carrabelle. GPS: 29.936631, -84.735089

18 • A3 | Tate's Hell SF - Doyle Creek

Dispersed sites, No water, Vault/pit toilet, Tent & RV camping: $10, Stay limit: 14 days, Open all year, Reservations not accepted, Elev: 33ft/10m, Tel: 850-697-3734, Nearest town: Carrabelle. GPS: 29.832616, -84.914369

19 • A3 | Tate's Hell SF - Dry Bridge

Dispersed sites, No water, Vault/pit toilet, Tent & RV camping: $10, Stay limit: 14 days, Open all year, Reservations not accepted, Elev: 39ft/12m, Tel: 850-697-3734, Nearest town: Carrabelle. GPS: 29.843373, -84.875389

20 • A3 | Tate's Hell SF - Gully Branch

Dispersed sites, No toilets, Tent & RV camping: $10, Stay limit: 14 days, Open all year, Reservations not accepted, Elev: 26ft/8m, Tel: 850-697-3734, Nearest town: Carrabelle. GPS: 29.959164, -84.719424

21 • A3 | Tate's Hell SF - Log Cabin #1

Dispersed sites, No water, Vault/pit toilet, Tent & RV camping: $10, Stay limit: 14 days, Open all year, Reservations not accepted, Elev: 36ft/11m, Tel: 850-697-3734, Nearest town: Sopchoppy. GPS: 30.032855, -84.595754

22 • A3 | Tate's Hell SF - Log Cabin #2

Dispersed sites, No water, Vault/pit toilet, Tent & RV camping: $10, Stay limit: 14 days, Open all year, Reservations not accepted, Elev: 52ft/16m, Tel: 850-697-3734, Nearest town: Sopchoppy. GPS: 30.032259, -84.594112

23 • A3 | Tate's Hell SF - Log Cabin #3

Dispersed sites, No water, Vault/pit toilet, Tent & RV camping: $10, Stay limit: 14 days, Open all year, Reservations not accepted, Elev: 49ft/15m, Tel: 850-697-3734, Nearest town: Sopchoppy. GPS: 30.027352, -84.588072

24 • A3 | Tate's Hell SF - Log Cabin #4

Dispersed sites, No water, Vault/pit toilet, Tent & RV camping: $10, Stay limit: 14 days, Open all year, Reservations not accepted, Elev: 56ft/17m, Tel: 850-697-3734, Nearest town: Sopchoppy. GPS: 30.027159, -84.587305

25 • A3 | Tate's Hell SF - Loop Road

Dispersed sites, No water, Vault/pit toilet, Tent & RV camping: $10, Stay limit: 14 days, Open all year, Reservations not accepted, Elev: 36ft/11m, Tel: 850-697-3734, Nearest town: Sopchoppy. GPS: 29.990141, -84.535531

26 • A3 | Tate's Hell SF - New River

Dispersed sites, No toilets, Tent & RV camping: $10, Nothing larger than van/PU, Stay limit: 14 days, Open all year, Reservations not accepted, Elev: 7ft/2m, Tel: 850-697-3734, Nearest town: Carrabelle. GPS: 29.931169, -84.735787

27 • A3 | Tate's Hell SF - New River Camp #2

Dispersed sites, No water, Vault/pit toilet, Tent & RV camping: $10, Stay limit: 14 days, Open all year, Reservations not accepted, Elev: 18ft/5m, Tel: 850-697-3734, Nearest town: Carrabelle. GPS: 29.963117, -84.723852

28 • A3 | Tate's Hell SF - New River Camp #3

Dispersed sites, No water, Vault/pit toilet, Tent & RV camping: $10, Stay limit: 14 days, Open all year, Reservations not accepted, Elev: 18ft/5m, Tel: 850-697-3734, Nearest town: Carrabelle. GPS: 29.971501, -84.726179

29 • A3 | Tate's Hell SF - New River Camp #4

Dispersed sites, No water, Vault/pit toilet, Tent & RV camping: $10, Stay limit: 14 days, Open all year, Reservations not accepted, Elev: 18ft/5m, Tel: 850-697-3734, Nearest town: Carrabelle. GPS: 29.977581, -84.729212

30 • A3 | Tate's Hell SF - New River Camp #5

Dispersed sites, No water, Vault/pit toilet, Tent & RV camping: $10, Stay limit: 14 days, Open all year, Reservations not accepted, Elev: 18ft/5m, Tel: 850-697-3734, Nearest town: Carrabelle. GPS: 29.982853, -84.733953

31 • A3 | Tate's Hell SF - New River Camp #6

Dispersed sites, No water, Vault/pit toilet, Tent & RV camping: $10, Stay limit: 14 days, Open all year, Reservations not accepted, Elev: 18ft/5m, Tel: 850-697-3734, Nearest town: Carrabelle. GPS: 29.989686, -84.738044

32 • A3 | Tate's Hell SF - New River Camp #7

Dispersed sites, No water, Vault/pit toilet, Tent & RV camping: $10, Stay limit: 14 days, Open all year, Reservations not accepted, Elev: 18ft/5m, Tel: 850-697-3734, Nearest town: Carrabelle. GPS: 29.993866, -84.745503

33 • A3 | Tate's Hell SF - Nick's Road

Dispersed sites, No water, Vault/pit toilet, Tent & RV camping: $10, Stay limit: 14 days, Open all year, Reservations not accepted, Elev: 46ft/14m, Tel: 850-697-3734, Nearest town: Sopchoppy. GPS: 30.013914, -84.577499

34 • A3 | Tate's Hell SF - North Road Camp

Dispersed sites, No water, Vault/pit toilet, Tent & RV camping: $10, Stay limit: 14 days, Open all year, Reservations not accepted, Elev: 46ft/14m, Tel: 850-697-3734, Nearest town: Carrabelle. GPS: 30.018197, -84.807979

35 • A3 | Tate's Hell SF - Parker Place

Dispersed sites, No water, Vault/pit toilet, Tent & RV camping: $10, Stay limit: 14 days, Open all year, Reservations not accepted, Elev: 33ft/10m, Tel: 850-697-3734, Nearest town: Carrabelle. GPS: 29.912032, -84.731094

36 • A3 | Tate's Hell SF - Pidcock Road

Dispersed sites, No water, No toilets, Tent & RV camping: $10, Stay limit: 14 days, Open all year, Reservations not accepted, Elev: 5ft/2m, Tel: 850-697-3734, Nearest town: Carrabelle. GPS: 29.819583, -84.825329

37 • A3 | Tate's Hell SF - Pope Place

Dispersed sites, No water, Vault/pit toilet, Tent & RV camping: $10, Stay limit: 14 days, Open all year, Reservations not accepted, Elev: 23ft/7m, Tel: 850-697-3734, Nearest town: Carrabelle. GPS: 29.896215, -84.733881

38 • A3 | Tate's Hell SF - Rake Creek

Dispersed sites, No toilets, Tent & RV camping: $10, Stay limit: 14 days, Open all year, Reservations not accepted, Elev: 6ft/2m, Tel: 850-697-3734, Nearest town: Carrabelle. GPS: 29.826731, -84.846319

39 • A3 | Tate's Hell SF - Rock Landing

Dispersed sites, No toilets, Tent & RV camping: $10, Also boat-in sites, Stay limit: 14 days, Open all year, Reservations not accepted, Elev: 43ft/13m, Tel: 850-697-3734, Nearest town: Sopchoppy. GPS: 29.979998, -84.568237

40 • A3 | Tate's Hell SF - Sunday Rollaway

Dispersed sites, No water, Vault/pit toilet, Tent & RV camping: $10, Stay limit: 14 days, Open all year, Reservations not accepted, Elev: 10ft/3m, Tel: 850-697-3734, Nearest town: Carrabelle. GPS: 29.903185, -84.651583

41 • A3 | Tate's Hell SF - Unnamed

Dispersed sites, No toilets, Tent & RV camping: $10, Stay limit: 14 days, Open all year, Reservations not accepted, Elev: 30ft/9m, Tel: 850-697-3734, Nearest town: Carrabelle. GPS: 30.031393, -84.828231

42 • A3 | Tate's Hell SF - Warren Bluff

Dispersed sites, No water, Vault/pit toilet, Tent & RV camping: $10, Stay limit: 14 days, Open all year, Reservations not accepted, Elev: 26ft/8m, Tel: 850-697-3734, Nearest town: Carrabelle. GPS: 29.874047, -84.696422

43 • A3 | Tate's Hell SF - Whiskey George

Dispersed sites, No water, Vault/pit toilet, Tent & RV camping: $10, Stay limit: 14 days, Open all year, Reservations not accepted, Elev: 36ft/11m, Tel: 850-697-3734, Nearest town: Carrabelle. GPS: 29.902288, -84.876369

44 • A3 | Tate's Hell SF - Womack Creek

Total sites: 12, RV sites: 12, No water, Flush toilet, Free showers, Tent & RV camping: $10, Stay limit: 14 days, Open all year, Reservations not accepted, Elev: 13ft/4m, Tel: 850-697-3734, Nearest town: Sopchoppy. GPS: 30.001591, -84.539113

45 • A4 | Cary SF

Total sites: 6, RV sites: 6, Elec sites: 6, Water at site, Flush toilet, Free showers, RV dump, Tent & RV camping: $14, Non-potable water, Group site, Stay limit: 14 days, Open all year, Max Length: 45ft, Reservations accepted, Elev: 78ft/24m, Tel: 904-266-5021, Nearest town: Bryceville. GPS: 30.398788, -81.927274

46 • B4 | Goethe SF - Black Prong

Dispersed sites, No water, Vault/pit toilet, Tent & RV camping: $10, Camping permit required, Elev: 52ft/16m, Tel: 352-465-8585, Nearest town: Dunellon. GPS: 29.306852, -82.596197

47 • B4 | Tiger Bay SF - Bennett Field

Total sites: 6, RV sites: 5, Elec sites: 0, No water, Vault/pit toilet, No showers, No RV dump, Tent & RV camping: $10, Stay limit: 14 days, Open all year, Max Length: 113ft, Reservations accepted, Elev: 56ft/17m, Tel: 386-226-0250, Nearest town: Deland. GPS: 29.189134, -81.167644

48 • B4 | Tiger Bay SF - Tram Road Equestrian

Total sites: 4, RV sites: 4, No water, Vault/pit toilet, No showers, No RV dump, Tent & RV camping: $10, Non-potable water, Stay limit: 14 days, Open all year, Reservations accepted, Elev: 46ft/14m, Tel: 386-226-0250, Nearest town: Deland. GPS: 29.228718, -81.182757

49 • B4 | Welaka SF - Arabian Rd Equestrian Camp

Dispersed sites, No water, Tent & RV camping: $10, Stay limit: 14 days, Open all year, Reservations accepted, Elev: 69ft/21m, Tel: 386-292-2478, Nearest town: Weleka. GPS: 29.469605, -81.651712

50 • B4 | Withlacoochee SF - Croom Motorcycle RA - Buttgenbach

Total sites: 51, RV sites: 51, Elec sites: 51, No water, Vault/pit toilet, Tent & RV camping: $25, Stay limit: 14 days, Open all year, Max Length: 77ft, Reservations accepted, Elev: 84ft/26m, Tel: 352-344-4238, Nearest town: Inverness. GPS: 28.567445, -82.242348

51 • B4 | Withlacoochee SF - Cypress Glen

Total sites: 34, RV sites: 33, Elec sites: 33, Water at site, Flush toilet, Free showers, No RV dump, Tents: $15-25/RVs: $25, Dump station at Silver Lake CG, Stay limit: 14 days, Open all year, Max Length: 55ft, Reservations accepted, Elev: 82ft/25m, Tel: 352-797-4140, Nearest town: Ridge Manor. GPS: 28.570917, -82.211336

52 • B4 | Withlacoochee SF - Hog Island

Total sites: 20, RV sites: 20, Central water, Flush toilet, Free showers, RV dump, Tent & RV camping: $15, Stay limit: 14 days, Open all year, Max Length: 55ft, Reservations accepted, Elev: 59ft/18m, Tel: 352-754-6896, Nearest town: Nobleton. GPS: 28.621143, -82.240848

53 • B4 | Withlacoochee SF - Holder Mine RA

Total sites: 27, RV sites: 27, Elec sites: 27, Water at site, Flush toilet, Free showers, RV dump, Tent & RV camping: $25, Stay limit: 14 days, Open all year, Max Length: 50ft, Reservations accepted, Elev: 62ft/19m, Tel: 352-797-4140, Nearest town: Inverness. GPS: 28.799781, -82.382253

54 • B4 | Withlacoochee SF - Mutual Mine RA

Total sites: 13, RV sites: 13, Central water, Vault/pit toilet, No showers, No RV dump, Tent & RV camping: $15, Stay limit: 14 days, Open all year, Max Length: 40ft, Reservations accepted, Elev: 66ft/20m, Tel: 352-797-4140, Nearest town: Flora City. GPS: 28.756464, -82.356429

55 • B4 | Withlacoochee SF - River Jct

Total sites: 20, RV sites: 20, Central water, Flush toilet, Free showers, No RV dump, Tent & RV camping: $10, Stay limit: 14 days, Open all year, Max Length: 45ft, Reservations accepted, Elev: 98ft/30m, Tel: 352-797-4140, Nearest town: Ridge Manor. GPS: 28.572926, -82.200749

56 • B4 | Withlacoochee SF - Silver Lake CG

Total sites: 23, RV sites: 23, Elec sites: 23, Water at site, Flush toilet, Free showers, RV dump, Tent & RV camping: $25, Stay limit: 14 days, Reservations accepted, Elev: 26ft/8m, Tel: 352-797-4140, Nearest town: Ridge Manor. GPS: 28.576455, -82.217886

57 • B4 | Withlacoochee SF - Tillis Hill Equestrian Camp

Total sites: 37, RV sites: 37, Elec sites: 37, Water at site, Flush toilet, Free showers, RV dump, Tent & RV camping: $25, Stay limit: 14 days, Open all year, Max Length: 64ft, Reservations required, Elev: 240ft/73m, Tel: 352-797-4140, Nearest town: Inverness. GPS: 28.727815, -82.414892

58 • B4 | Withlacoochee SF - Two Mile Prairie - Bear Head Hammock

Total sites: 3, RV sites: 3, No water, Vault/pit toilet, No showers, No RV dump, Tent & RV camping: $10, Open all year, Max Length: 60ft, Reservations accepted, Elev: 59ft/18m, Tel: 352-797-4140, Nearest town: Hernando. GPS: 28.969925, -82.401695

59 • C4 | Lake Wales Ridge SF - Reedy Creek

Total sites: 8, RV sites: 4, No water, No toilets, No showers, No RV dump, Tent & RV camping: $10, Stay limit: 14 days, Open all year, Reservations accepted, Elev: 108ft/33m, Tel: 863-589-0545, Nearest town: Frostproof. GPS: 27.705564, -81.444671

60 • C4 | Lakes Wales Ridge SF - Reedy Creek II Hunt Cmp

Total sites: 10, RV sites: 10, No water, No toilets, Tent & RV camping: $9, Vault toilet across street at Reedy Creek CG, Stay limit: 14 days, Open all year, Reservations not accepted, Elev: 118ft/36m, Tel: 863-635-7801, Nearest town: Frostproof. GPS: 27.705646, -81.446478

61 • C4 | Lakes Wales Ridge SF - Walk-in-the-Water

Total sites: 10, RV sites: 8, No water, Vault/pit toilet, No showers, No RV dump, Tent & RV camping: $9, Stay limit: 14 days, Reservations required, Elev: 89ft/27m, Tel: 863-589-0545, Nearest town: Frostproof. GPS: 27.783018, -81.448737

62 • C4 | Myakka SF - Flying A

Total sites: 10, RV sites: 5, No water, Vault/pit toilet, Tent & RV camping: $10, Stay limit: 14 days, Max Length: 24ft, Reservations accepted, Elev: 16ft/5m, Tel: 941-460-1333, Nearest town: North Port. GPS: 26.984696, -82.280297

63 • C4 | Okaloacoochie Slough SF - Wild Cow

Dispersed sites, No water, No toilets, Tent & RV camping: Free, Open all year, Elev: 43ft/13m, Tel: 863-612-0776, Nearest town: Felda. GPS: 26.527205, -81.320913

Illinois

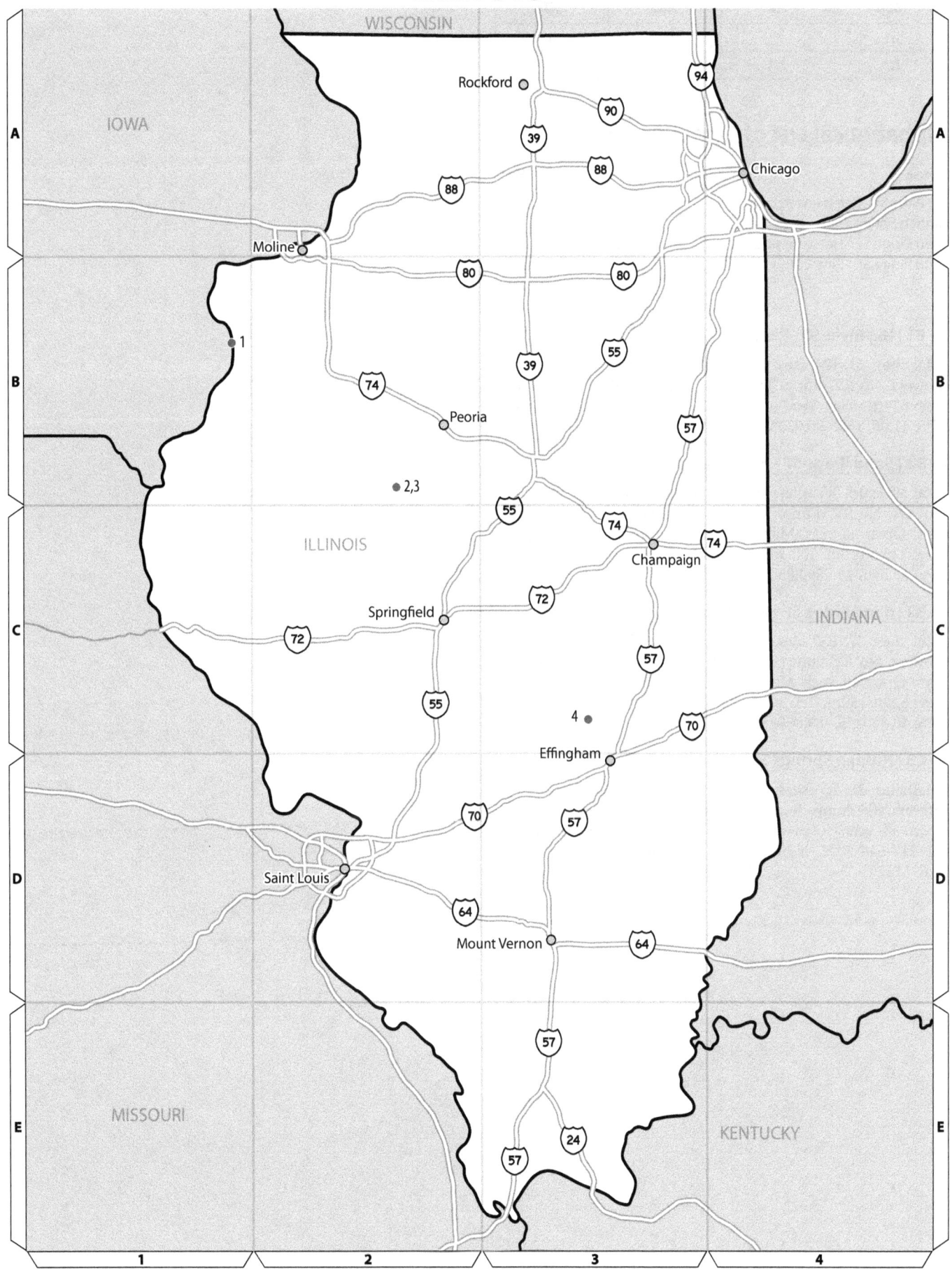

Map	ID	Map	ID
B1	1	C3	4
B2	2-3		

Alphabetical List of Camping Areas

Name	ID	Map
Big River SF - Riverview Access	1	B1
Hidden Springs SF	4	C3
Sand Ridge SF - Horse Camp	2	B2
Sand Ridge SF - Pine Camp	3	B2

1 • B1 | Big River SF - Riverview Access

Total sites: 63, RV sites: 63, Central water, Vault/pit toilet, No showers, No RV dump, Tent & RV camping: $8, Open all year, Elev: 574ft/175m, Tel: 309-374-2496, Nearest town: Keithsburg. GPS: 41.051135, -90.935551

2 • B2 | Sand Ridge SF - Horse Camp

Total sites: 16, RV sites: 16, Central water, Vault/pit toilet, No showers, No RV dump, Tent & RV camping: $8, Stay limit: 14 days, Open all year, Max Length: 55ft, Reservations accepted, Elev: 525ft/160m, Tel: 309-597-2212, Nearest town: Forest City. GPS: 40.390746, -89.885424

3 • B2 | Sand Ridge SF - Pine Camp

Total sites: 27, RV sites: 27, Central water, Vault/pit toilet, No showers, No RV dump, Tent & RV camping: $8, Stay limit: 14 days, Open all year, Max Length: 52ft, Reservations accepted, Elev: 522ft/159m, Tel: 309-597-2212, Nearest town: Forest City. GPS: 40.390225, -89.868259

4 • C3 | Hidden Springs SF

Total sites: 28, RV sites: 28, Central water, Vault/pit toilet, No showers, RV dump, Tent & RV camping: $8, Stay limit: 14 days, Open all year, Reservations not accepted, Elev: 630ft/192m, Tel: 217-644-3091, Nearest town: Strasburg. GPS: 39.316438, -88.691157

Indiana

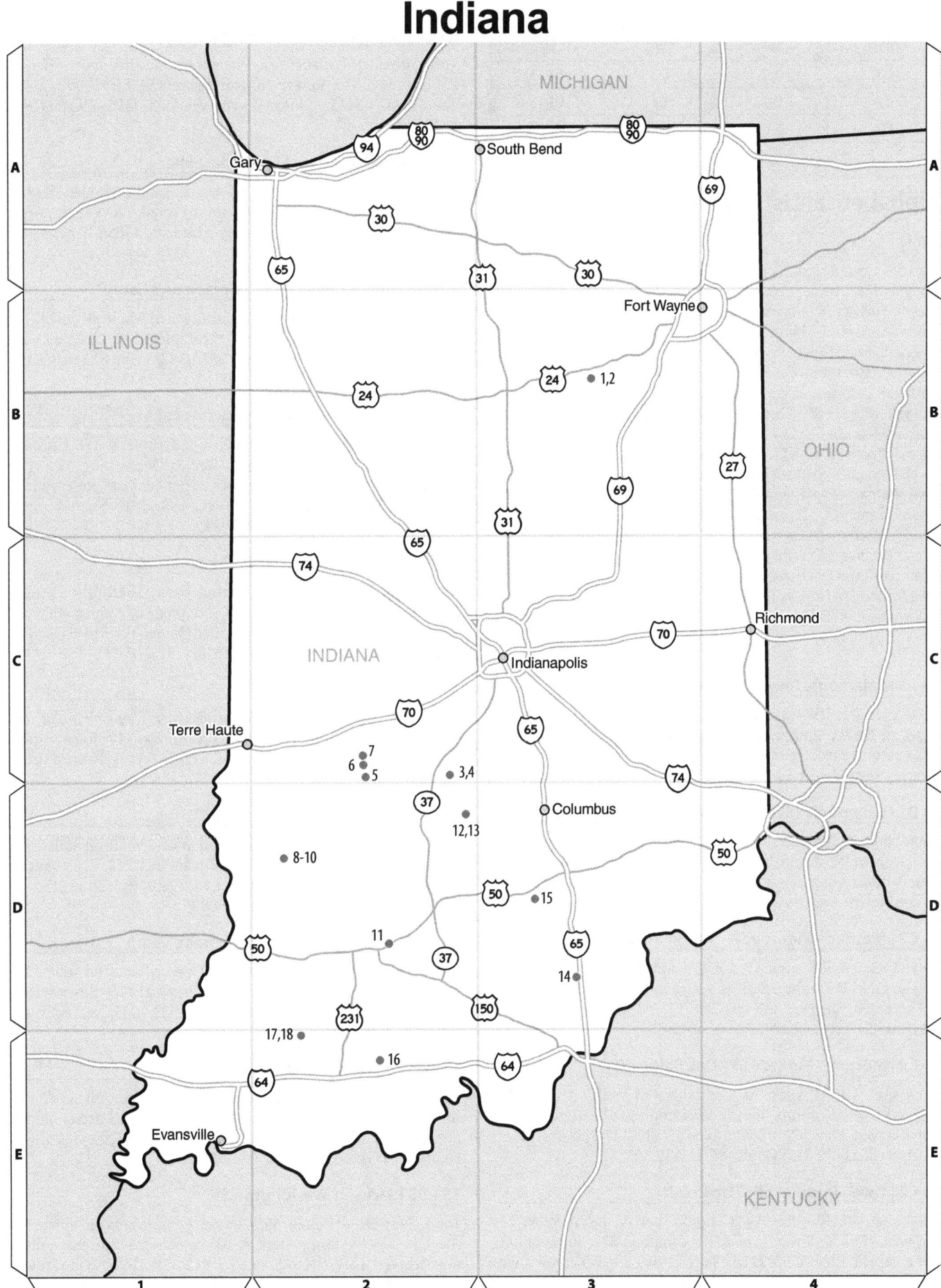

Map	ID	Map	ID
B3	1-2	D3	14-15
C2	3-7	E2	16-18
D2	8-13		

Alphabetical List of Camping Areas

Name	ID	Map
Clark SF - Horse Camp	14	D3
Ferdinand SF	16	E2
Greene-Sullivan SF - Horseman's Camp	8	D2
Greene-Sullivan SF - Narrow Lake	9	D2
Greene-Sullivan SF - Reservoir 26	10	D2
Jackson-Washington SF	15	D3
Martin SF	11	D2
Morgan - Monroe SF - Mason Ridge CG	3	C2
Morgan - Monroe SF - Oak Ridge CG	4	C2
Owen Putnam SF - Fish Creek	5	C2
Owen Putnam SF - Horse Camp	6	C2
Owen Putnam SF - Rattlesnake	7	C2
Pike SF - Family CG	17	E2
Pike SF - Horseman's Camp	18	E2
Salamonie River SF - Family CG	1	B3
Salamonie River SF - Horseman's Camp	2	B3
Yellowwood SF - Family CG	12	D2
Yellowwood SF - Horseman's Camp	13	D2

1 • B3 | Salamonie River SF - Family CG

Total sites: 21, RV sites: 21, Central water, Vault/pit toilet, No showers, No RV dump, Tent & RV camping: $12, Open all year, Reservations not accepted, Elev: 837ft/255m, Tel: 260-468-2125, Nearest town: Andrews. GPS: 40.808249, -85.690313

2 • B3 | Salamonie River SF - Horseman's Camp

Total sites: 15, RV sites: 15, Central water, Vault/pit toilet, No showers, No RV dump, Tent & RV camping: $13, Open all year, Reservations not accepted, Elev: 787ft/240m, Tel: 260-468-2125, Nearest town: Andrews. GPS: 40.812521, -85.696163

3 • C2 | Morgan - Monroe SF - Mason Ridge CG

Total sites: 19, RV sites: 19, Central water, Vault/pit toilet, No showers, No RV dump, Tent & RV camping: $12, Reservations not accepted, Elev: 951ft/290m, Tel: 765-342-4026, Nearest town: Martinsville. GPS: 39.328574, -86.424595

4 • C2 | Morgan - Monroe SF - Oak Ridge CG

Total sites: 10, RV sites: 10, Central water, Vault/pit toilet, No showers, No RV dump, Tent & RV camping: $12, Reservations not accepted, Elev: 920ft/280m, Tel: 765-342-4026, Nearest town: Martinsville. GPS: 39.334355, -86.419536

5 • C2 | Owen Putnam SF - Fish Creek

Total sites: 14, RV sites: 14, Central water, Vault/pit toilet, No showers, No RV dump, Tent & RV camping: $12, Reservations not accepted, Elev: 705ft/215m, Tel: 812-829-2462, Nearest town: Vandalia. GPS: 39.319785, -86.847246

6 • C2 | Owen Putnam SF - Horse Camp

Total sites: 15, RV sites: 15, No water, Vault/pit toilet, Tent & RV camping: $15, Reservations not accepted, Elev: 899ft/274m, Tel: 812-829-2462, Nearest town: Vandalia. GPS: 39.369018, -86.857125

7 • C2 | Owen Putnam SF - Rattlesnake

Total sites: 11, RV sites: 11, No water, Vault/pit toilet, Tent & RV camping: $12, Reservations not accepted, Elev: 873ft/266m, Tel: 812-829-2462, Nearest town: Vandalia. GPS: 39.399438, -86.856664

8 • D2 | Greene-Sullivan SF - Horseman's Camp

Total sites: 20, RV sites: 20, Central water, Vault/pit toilet, No showers, No RV dump, Tent & RV camping: $12, Open all year, Reservations not accepted, Elev: 597ft/182m, Tel: 812-648-2810, Nearest town: Dugger. GPS: 39.002147, -87.254756

9 • D2 | Greene-Sullivan SF - Narrow Lake

Total sites: 5, RV sites: 5, Elec sites: 5, Central water, Vault/pit toilet, No showers, No RV dump, Tent & RV camping: $20, Also cabins, Also 18 Rent-a-Camp sites, Open all year, Reservations accepted, Elev: 545ft/166m, Tel: 812-648-2810, Nearest town: Dugger. GPS: 39.033655, -87.257974

10 • D2 | Greene-Sullivan SF - Reservoir 26

Total sites: 25, RV sites: 25, Central water, Vault/pit toilet, No showers, RV dump, Tent & RV camping: $8, Open all year, Reservations not accepted, Elev: 502ft/153m, Tel: 812-648-2810, Nearest town: Dugger. GPS: 39.018389, -87.241929

11 • D2 | Martin SF

Total sites: 26, RV sites: 26, Central water, Vault/pit toilet, No showers, No RV dump, Tent & RV camping: $12, Reservations not accepted, Elev: 750ft/229m, Tel: 812-247-3491, Nearest town: Shoals. GPS: 38.699251, -86.723741

12 • D2 | Yellowwood SF - Family CG

Total sites: 80, RV sites: 80, Central water, Vault/pit toilet, No showers, No RV dump, Tent & RV camping: $12, Reservations not accepted, Elev: 627ft/191m, Tel: 812-988-7945, Nearest town: Nashville. GPS: 39.180545, -86.336885

13 • D2 | Yellowwood SF - Horseman's Camp

Total sites: 10, RV sites: 10, Central water, Vault/pit toilet, No showers, No RV dump, Tent & RV camping: $15, Reservations not accepted, Elev: 636ft/194m, Tel: 812-988-7945, Nearest town: Nashville. GPS: 39.177747, -86.335021

14 • D3 | Clark SF - Horse Camp

Total sites: 26, RV sites: 26, Central water, Vault/pit toilet, No showers, No RV dump, Tent & RV camping: $19-25, Reservations not accepted, Elev: 670ft/204m, Tel: 812-294-4306, Nearest town: Henryville. GPS: 38.572972, -85.793963

15 • D3 | Jackson-Washington SF

Total sites: 56, RV sites: 56, Central water, Vault/pit toilet, No showers, No RV dump, Tent & RV camping: $13, Reservations not accepted, Elev: 742ft/226m, Tel: 812-358-2160, Nearest town: Brownstone. GPS: 38.865059, -86.001228

16 • E2 | Ferdinand SF

Total sites: 69, RV sites: 69, Central water, Vault/pit toilet, No showers, No RV dump, Tent & RV camping: $8, Reservations not accepted, Elev: 528ft/161m, Tel: 812-367-1524, Nearest town: Ferdinand. GPS: 38.253841, -86.770216

17 • E2 | Pike SF - Family CG

Total sites: 11, RV sites: 11, Central water, Vault/pit toilet, No showers, No RV dump, Tent & RV camping: $12, Reservations not accepted, Elev: 510ft/155m, Tel: 812-367-1524, Nearest town: Winslow. GPS: 38.355096, -87.155046

18 • E2 | Pike SF - Horseman's Camp

Total sites: 25, RV sites: 25, Central water, No showers, No RV dump, Tent & RV camping: $13, Reservations not accepted, Elev: 545ft/166m, Tel: 812-367-1524, Nearest town: Winslow. GPS: 38.358357, -87.160377

Iowa

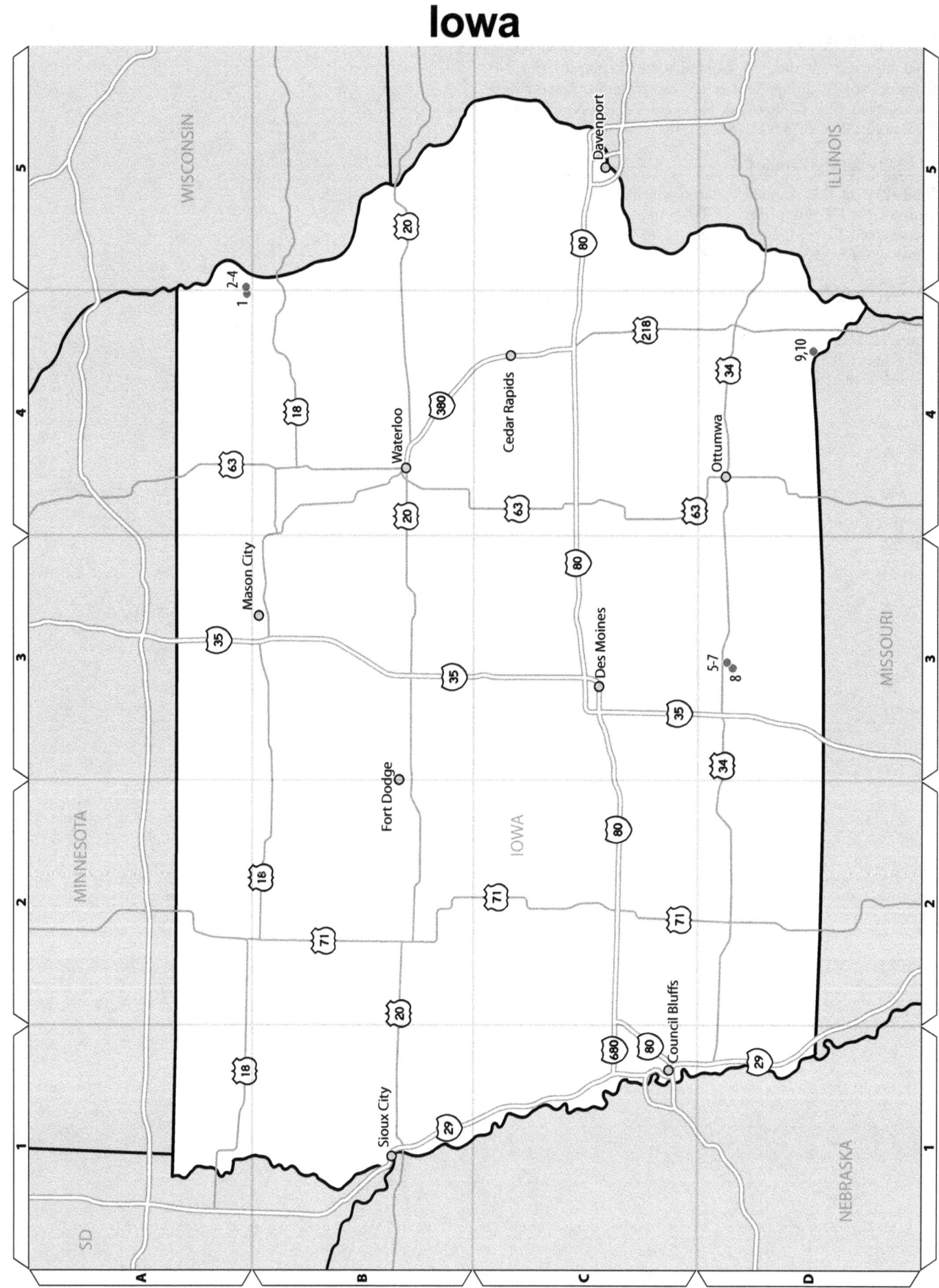

Map	ID	Map	ID
A4	1	D3	5-8
A5	2-4	D4	9-10

Alphabetical List of Camping Areas

Name	ID	Map
Shimek SF - Lick Creek Lower Equestrian	9	D4
Shimek SF - Lick Creek Upper CG	10	D4
Stephens SF - Lucas - Middle	5	D3
Stephens SF - Lucas - Mine Pond	6	D3
Stephens SF - Lucas - Primitive	7	D3
Stephens SF - Whitebreast Equestrian	8	D3
Yellow River SF - Big Paint Creek	1	A4
Yellow River SF - Creekside Equestrian	2	A5
Yellow River SF - Frontier Equestrian	3	A5
Yellow River SF - Little Paint Creek	4	A5

1 • A4 | Yellow River SF - Big Paint Creek

Total sites: 27, RV sites: 27, No water, Vault/pit toilet, Tent & RV camping: $6-12, Open all year, Max Length: 90ft, Reservations accepted, Elev: 768ft/234m, Tel: 563-586-2254, Nearest town: Harpers Ferry. GPS: 43.173912, -91.252416

2 • A5 | Yellow River SF - Creekside Equestrian

Total sites: 13, RV sites: 13, No water, Vault/pit toilet, Tent & RV camping: $10-16, Open all year, Max Length: 125ft, Reservations accepted, Elev: 856ft/261m, Tel: 563-586-2254, Nearest town: Harpers ferry. GPS: 43.177087, -91.229012

3 • A5 | Yellow River SF - Frontier Equestrian

Total sites: 20, RV sites: 20, No water, Vault/pit toilet, Tent & RV camping: $10-16, Open all year, Max Length: 90ft, Reservations accepted, Elev: 702ft/214m, Tel: 563-586-2254, Nearest town: Harpers ferry. GPS: 43.176889, -91.224006

4 • A5 | Yellow River SF - Little Paint Creek

Total sites: 71, RV sites: 71, No water, Vault/pit toilet, Tent & RV camping: $6-9, Youth group site: $20, Max Length: 80ft, Reservations accepted, Elev: 712ft/217m, Tel: 563-586-2254, Nearest town: Harpers Ferry. GPS: 43.181794, -91.235535

5 • D3 | Stephens SF - Lucas - Middle

Total sites: 9, RV sites: 9, Central water, Vault/pit toilet, No showers, No RV dump, Tent & RV camping: $6-9, Open all year, Max Length: 40ft, Elev: 1053ft/321m, Tel: 641-774-5632, Nearest town: Lucas. GPS: 41.017695, -93.485221

6 • D3 | Stephens SF - Lucas - Mine Pond

Total sites: 10, RV sites: 10, No water, Vault/pit toilet, Tent & RV camping: $6-9, Open all year, Max Length: 40ft, Elev: 945ft/288m, Tel: 641-774-5632, Nearest town: Lucas. GPS: 41.013778, -93.480964

7 • D3 | Stephens SF - Lucas - Primitive

Total sites: 8, RV sites: 8, Central water, No toilets, No showers, No RV dump, Tent & RV camping: $6-9, Vault toilet at Middle CG, Open all year, Max Length: 55ft, Reservations accepted, Elev: 1053ft/321m, Tel: 641-774-5632, Nearest town: Lucas. GPS: 41.005222, -93.483254

8 • D3 | Stephens SF - Whitebreast Equestrian

Total sites: 40, RV sites: 40, Central water, Vault/pit toilet, No showers, No RV dump, Tent & RV camping: $10-13, Open all year, Max Length: 65ft, Reservations accepted, Elev: 1063ft/324m, Tel: 641-774-5632, Nearest town: Lucas. GPS: 40.987734, -93.505779

9 • D4 | Shimek SF - Lick Creek Lower Equestrian

Total sites: 25, RV sites: 25, Central water, Vault/pit toilet, Tent & RV camping: $10, Equestrian, Open all year, Reservations accepted, Elev: 594ft/181m, Tel: 319-878-3811, Nearest town: Farmington. GPS: 40.610240, -91.672558

10 • D4 | Shimek SF - Lick Creek Upper CG

Total sites: 12, RV sites: 12, Central water, Vault/pit toilet, Tent & RV camping: $12, Equestrian, Open all year, Reservations accepted, Elev: 696ft/212m, Tel: 319-878-3811, Nearest town: Farmington. GPS: 40.618229, -91.679771

Louisiana

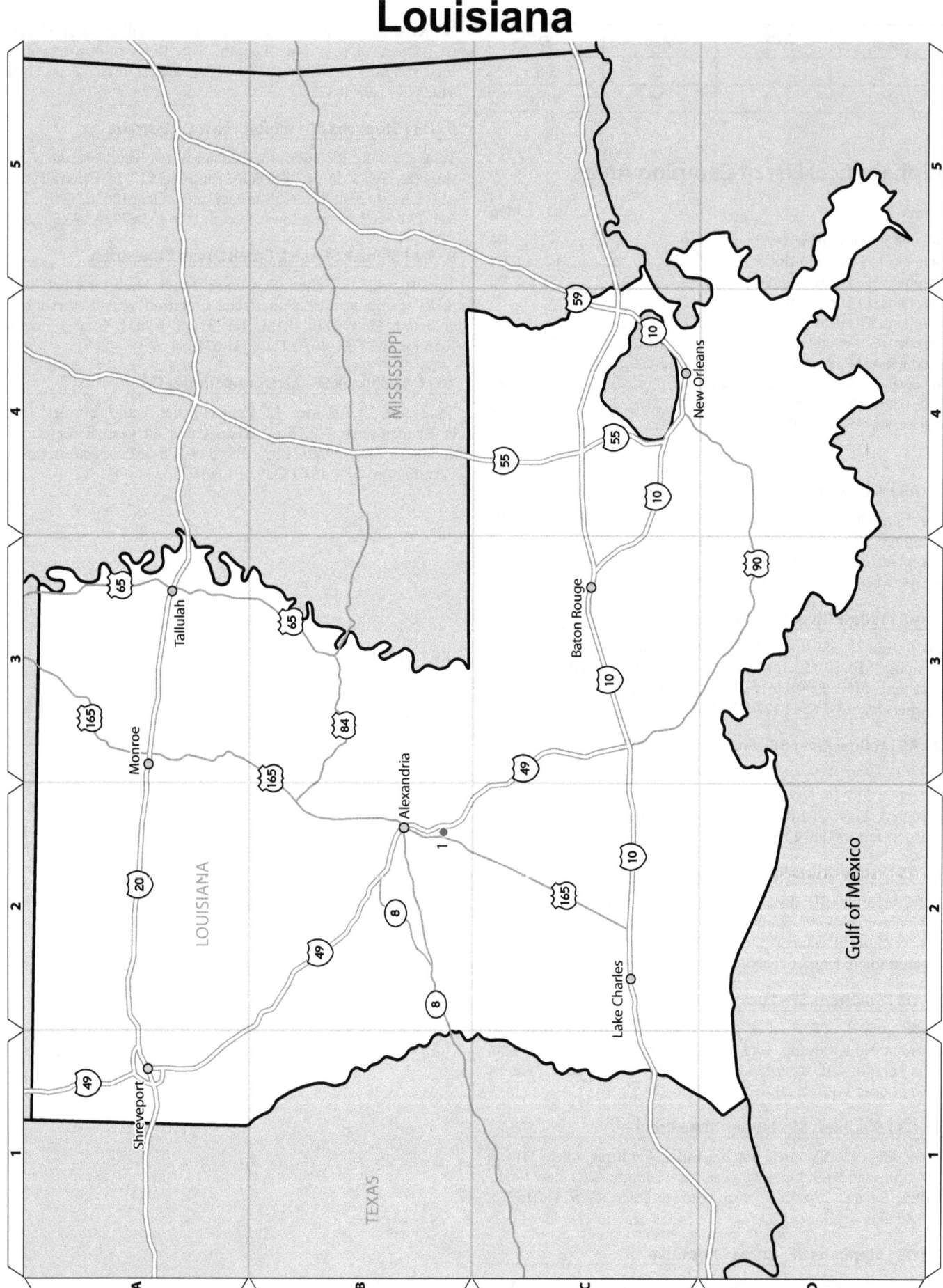

Map	ID	Map	ID
B2	1		

Alphabetical List of Camping Areas

Name   **ID**   **Map**

Alexander SF - Indian Creek .... 1 .... B2

1 • B2 | Alexander SF - Indian Creek

Total sites: 109, RV sites: 101, Elec sites: 101, Water at site, Flush toilet, Free showers, RV dump, Tents: $14/RVs: $22-28, Lower rates Nov-Feb, Open all year, Reservations accepted, Elev: 144ft/44m, Tel: 318-487-5058, Nearest town: Woodworth. GPS: 31.114631, -92.471261

Maryland

Map	ID	Map	ID
A1	1-6	B1	8-9
A2	7	C3	10-11

Alphabetical List of Camping Areas

Name	ID	Map
Cedarville SF - Equestrian	10	C3
Cedarville SF - Family CG	11	C3
Green Ridge SF	7	A2
Potomac SF - Laurel Run	8	B1
Potomac SF - Lostland Run	1	A1
Potomac SF - Wallman CG	9	B1
Savage River SF - Big Run Road 123-144	2	A1
Savage River SF - Blue Lick 164-168	3	A1
Savage River SF - Elk Lick 100-105	4	A1
Savage River SF - Swift River Road 106-113	5	A1
Savage River SF - Whitewater 114-122	6	A1

1 • A1 | Potomac SF - Lostland Run

Total sites: 6, No water, No toilets, Tent & RV camping: $10, Open all year, Elev: 2405ft/733m, Tel: 301-334-2038, Nearest town: Oakland. GPS: 39.378212, -79.272338

2 • A1 | Savage River SF - Big Run Road 123-144

Dispersed sites, No water, No toilets, Tent & RV camping: $10, 19 sites along road, Elev: 1803ft/550m, Tel: 301-895-5759, Nearest town: Grantsville. GPS: 39.567982, -79.155808

3 • A1 | Savage River SF - Blue Lick 164-168

Total sites: 5, RV sites: 5, No water, No toilets, Tent & RV camping: $10, Dispersed sites along road, Elev: 2323ft/708m, Tel: 301-895-5759, Nearest town: Grantsville. GPS: 39.647207, -79.066509

4 • A1 | Savage River SF - Elk Lick 100-105

Total sites: 6, RV sites: 6, No water, No toilets, Tent & RV camping: $10, Dispersed sites along road, Elev: 2244ft/684m, Tel: 301-895-5759, Nearest town: Grantsville. GPS: 39.609365, -79.102224

5 • A1 | Savage River SF - Swift River Road 106-113

Dispersed sites, No water, No toilets, Tent & RV camping: $10, 7 sites along road, Elev: 1722ft/525m, Tel: 301-895-5759, Nearest town: Grantsville. GPS: 39.575246, -79.096616

6 • A1 | Savage River SF - Whitewater 114-122

Total sites: 9, No water, No toilets, Tent & RV camping: $10, Elev: 1368ft/417m, Tel: 301-895-5759, Nearest town: Grantsville. GPS: 39.502454, -79.122145

7 • A2 | Green Ridge SF

Total sites: 100, RV sites: 100, No toilets, Tent & RV camping: $10, Sites dispersed, Permit required, Open all year, Elev: 958ft/292m, Tel: 301-478-3124, Nearest town: Flintstone. GPS: 39.665451, -78.441545

8 • B1 | Potomac SF - Laurel Run

Total sites: 8, No water, No toilets, Tent & RV camping: $10, Open all year, Elev: 2290ft/698m, Tel: 301-334-2038, Nearest town: Oakland. GPS: 39.346177, -79.277141

9 • B1 | Potomac SF - Wallman CG

Total sites: 8, No water, No toilets, Tent & RV camping: $10, Open all year, Elev: 2277ft/694m, Tel: 301-334-2038, Nearest town: Oakland. GPS: 39.326383, -79.279339

10 • C3 | Cedarville SF - Equestrian

Total sites: 5, RV sites: 5, Water available, Flush toilet, Free showers, No RV dump, Tent & RV camping: $23, Open Apr-Oct, Elev: 207ft/63m, Tel: 301-888-1410, Nearest town: Brandywine. GPS: 38.648829, -76.812672

11 • C3 | Cedarville SF - Family CG

Total sites: 27, RV sites: 27, Elec sites: 9, Water available, Flush toilet, Free showers, No RV dump, Tents: $19/RVs: $25, Open Apr-Oct, Reservations accepted, Elev: 213ft/65m, Tel: 301-888-1410, Nearest town: Brandywine. GPS: 38.649953, -76.812962

Massachusetts

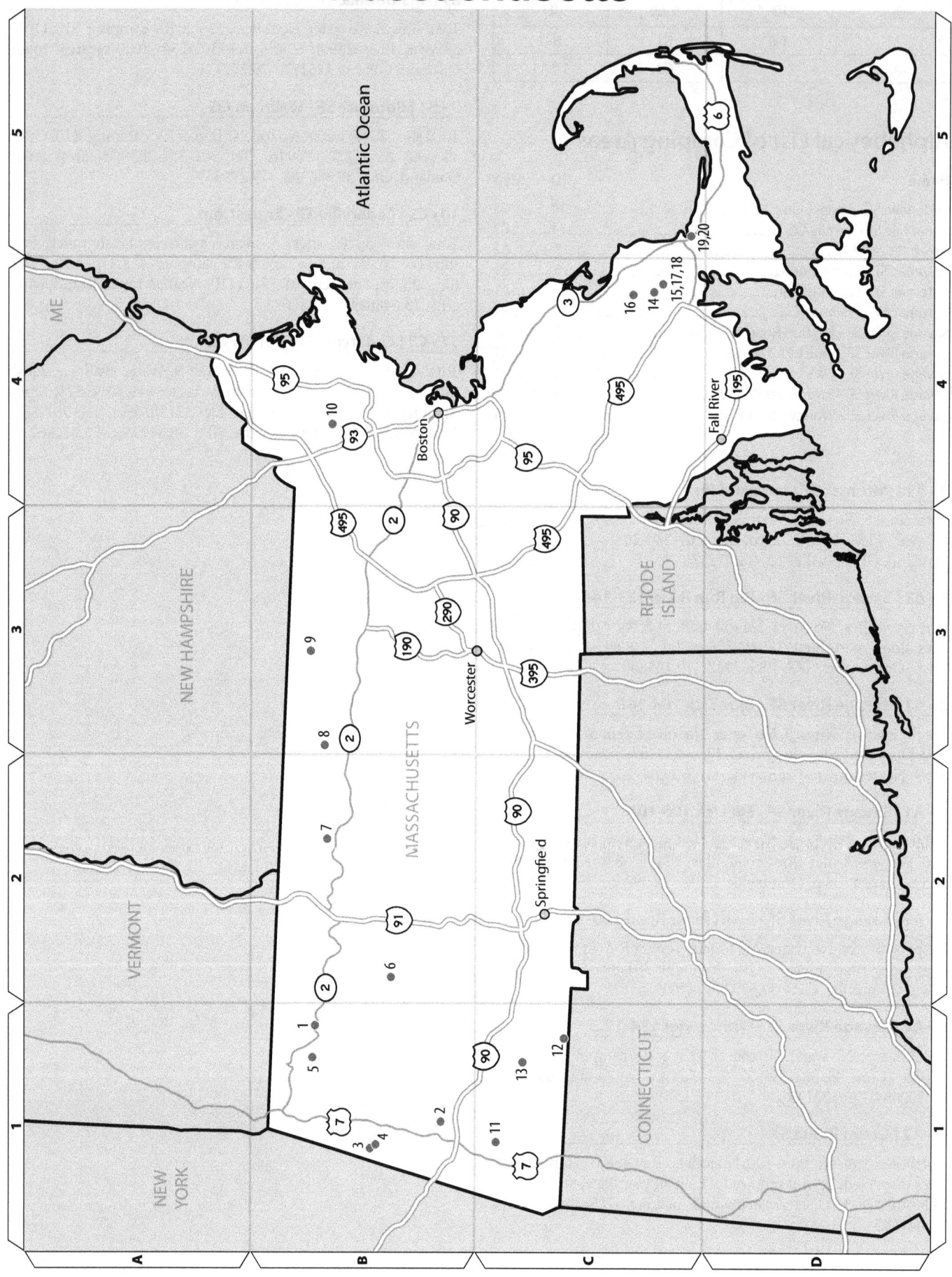

Map	ID	Map	ID
B1	1-5	C1	11-13
B2	6-7	C4	14-18
B3	8-9	C5	19-20
B4	10		

Alphabetical List of Camping Areas

Name	ID	Map
Beartown SF	11	C1
DAR SF	6	B2
Erving SF	7	B2
Granville SF	12	C1
Harold Parker SF - Lorraine Park	10	B4
Mohawk Trail SF	1	B1
Myles Standish SF - Barretts Pond #1	14	C4
Myles Standish SF - Charge Pond	15	C4
Myles Standish SF - Curlew Pond	16	C4
Myles Standish SF - Fearing Pond #1	17	C4
Myles Standish SF - Fearing Pond #2	18	C4
October Mountain SF	2	B1
Otter River SF	8	B3
Pittsfield SF - Berry Pond	3	B1
Pittsfield SF - Parker Brook	4	B1
Savoy Mountain SF	5	B1
Shawme Crowell SF - Area 1	19	C5
Shawme Crowell SF - Area 2	20	C5
Tolland SF	13	C1
Willard Brook SF	9	B3

1 • B1 | Mohawk Trail SF

Total sites: 44, RV sites: 36, Central water, Flush toilet, Free showers, No RV dump, Tent & RV camping: $54, Also group sites & cabins, Group site: $100 ($35 for MA residents), MA residents: $17, No pets, Register at Erving SF, Open Apr-Oct, Max Length: 30ft, Reservations accepted, Elev: 886ft/270m, Tel: 413-339-5504, Nearest town: Charlemont. GPS: 42.641602, -72.941406

2 • B1 | October Mountain SF

Total sites: 47, RV sites: 47, Central water, Flush toilet, Free showers, RV dump, Tent & RV camping: $54, MA residents: $17, Open May-Oct, Max Length: 34ft, Elev: 1079ft/329m, Tel: 413-243-1778, Nearest town: Leesville. GPS: 42.336386, -73.233573

3 • B1 | Pittsfield SF - Berry Pond

Total sites: 13, RV sites: 3, No water, Vault/pit toilet, Tent & RV camping: $54, MA residents: $17, Open May-Oct, Max Length: 35ft, Reservations accepted, Elev: 2080ft/634m, Tel: 413-442-8992, Nearest town: Pittsfield. GPS: 42.505168, -73.320668

4 • B1 | Pittsfield SF - Parker Brook

Total sites: 13, RV sites: 13, Central water, No toilets, No showers, Tent & RV camping: $40, $14 for MA residents, Open May-Oct, Elev: 1375ft/419m, Tel: 413-442-8992, Nearest town: Pittsfield. GPS: 42.489781, -73.304224

5 • B1 | Savoy Mountain SF

Total sites: 45, RV sites: 45, Central water, Flush toilet, Free showers, RV dump, Tent & RV camping: $54, Also cabins, MA residents: $17, Open May-Oct, Max Length: 35ft, Elev: 1972ft/601m, Tel: 413-663-8469, Nearest town: North Adams. GPS: 42.646841, -73.046639

6 • B2 | DAR SF

Total sites: 51, RV sites: 51, Central water, Flush toilet, Free showers, Tent & RV camping: $54, MA residents: $17, Group site $100/$35 for MA residents, Open May-Oct, Max Length: 54ft, Reservations accepted, Elev: 1486ft/453m, Tel: 413-268-7098, Nearest town: Goshen. GPS: 42.460205, -72.792725

7 • B2 | Erving SF

Total sites: 29, RV sites: 29, Central water, No toilets, No showers, No RV dump, Tent & RV camping: $54, MA residents: $17, Open May-Sep, Max Length: 14ft, Reservations accepted, Elev: 926ft/282m, Tel: 978-544-3939, Nearest town: Erving. GPS: 42.619532, -72.368447

8 • B3 | Otter River SF

Total sites: 75, RV sites: 17, Central water, Flush toilet, Free showers, No RV dump, Tent & RV camping: $54, MA residents: $17, Open May-Oct, Max Length: 28ft, Reservations accepted, Elev: 912ft/278m, Tel: 978-939-8962, Nearest town: Baldwinville. GPS: 42.626333, -72.079057

9 • B3 | Willard Brook SF

Total sites: 19, RV sites: 12, Central water, No toilets, No showers, No RV dump, Tent & RV camping: $40, MA residents: $14, Beware of your GPS guidance. The entrance is off Route 119, not Hosmer Road., Open May-Sep, Max Length: 35ft, Reservations accepted, Elev: 699ft/213m, Tel: 978-597-8802, Nearest town: Townsend. GPS: 42.660852, -71.789996

10 • B4 | Harold Parker SF - Lorraine Park

Total sites: 89, RV sites: 89, Elec sites: 10, Central water, No toilets, No showers, RV dump, Tents: $54/RVs: $54-60, MA residents: $17, No pets, Register at Erving SF, Open May-Sep, Max Length: 40ft, Reservations accepted, Elev: 134ft/41m, Tel: 978-475-7972, Nearest town: Andover. GPS: 42.608187, -71.092649

11 • C1 | Beartown SF

Total sites: 12, RV sites: 3, Central water, Vault/pit toilet, No showers, No RV dump, Tent & RV camping: $40, MA residents: $14, Open all year, Max Length: 25ft, Elev: 1608ft/490m, Tel: 413-528-0904, Nearest town: Monterey. GPS: 42.205346, -73.291723

12 • C1 | Granville SF

Total sites: 22, RV sites: 17, Central water, Flush toilet, Free showers, No RV dump, Tent & RV camping: $54, MA residents: $17, Open May-Oct, Max Length: 25ft, Reservations accepted, Elev: 1204ft/367m, Tel: 413-357-6611, Nearest town: Granville. GPS: 42.051848, -72.970545

13 • C1 | Tolland SF

Total sites: 91, RV sites: 48, Central water, Flush toilet, Free showers, RV dump, Tent & RV camping: $54, MA residents: $17, Open May-Sep, Max Length: 35ft, Reservations accepted,

Elev: 1532ft/467m, Tel: 413-269-6002, Nearest town: Otis. GPS: 42.145886, -73.044023

14 • C4 | Myles Standish SF - Barretts Pond #1

Total sites: 32, RV sites: 32, Central water, RV dump, Tent & RV camping: $54, MA residents: $17, Open Apr-Oct, Max Length: 30ft, Reservations accepted, Elev: 144ft/44m, Tel: 508-866-2526, Nearest town: South Carver. GPS: 41.845639, -70.691476

15 • C4 | Myles Standish SF - Charge Pond

Total sites: 223, RV sites: 223, Central water, Flush toilet, Free showers, RV dump, Tent & RV camping: $54, MA residents: $17, Group site $50/$35 for MA residents, Open Apr-Oct, Max Length: 30ft, Reservations accepted, Elev: 115ft/35m, Tel: 508-866-2526, Nearest town: South Carver. GPS: 41.817325, -70.673455

16 • C4 | Myles Standish SF - Curlew Pond

Total sites: 81, RV sites: 81, Central water, Flush toilet, Free showers, RV dump, Tent & RV camping: $54, MA residents: $17, Open Apr-Oct, Max Length: 30ft, Reservations accepted, Elev: 167ft/51m, Tel: 508-866-2526, Nearest town: South Carver. GPS: 41.893196, -70.698366

17 • C4 | Myles Standish SF - Fearing Pond #1

Total sites: 43, RV sites: 43, Central water, Flush toilet, Free showers, RV dump, Tent & RV camping: $54, MA residents: $17, Open Apr-Oct, Max Length: 30ft, Reservations accepted, Elev: 151ft/46m, Tel: 508-866-2526, Nearest town: South Carver. GPS: 41.827618, -70.664988

18 • C4 | Myles Standish SF - Fearing Pond #2

Total sites: 29, RV sites: 29, Central water, Flush toilet, Free showers, RV dump, Tent & RV camping: $54, MA residents: $17, Open Apr-Oct, Max Length: 30ft, Reservations accepted, Elev: 138ft/42m, Tel: 508-866-2526, Nearest town: South Carver. GPS: 41.833103, -70.668239

19 • C5 | Shawme Crowell SF - Area 1

Total sites: 47, RV sites: 47, Central water, Flush toilet, Free showers, RV dump, Tent & RV camping: $54, MA residents: $17, Stay limit: 14 days, Open Apr-Oct, Max Length: 30ft, Reservations accepted, Elev: 115ft/35m, Tel: 508-888-0351, Nearest town: Sandwich. GPS: 41.762867, -70.523564

20 • C5 | Shawme Crowell SF - Area 2

Total sites: 112, RV sites: 112, Central water, Flush toilet, Free showers, RV dump, Tent & RV camping: $54, MA residents: $17, Stay limit: 14 days, Open Apr-Oct, Max Length: 30ft, Reservations accepted, Elev: 144ft/44m, Tel: 508-888-0351, Nearest town: Sandwich. GPS: 41.755583, -70.516267

Michigan

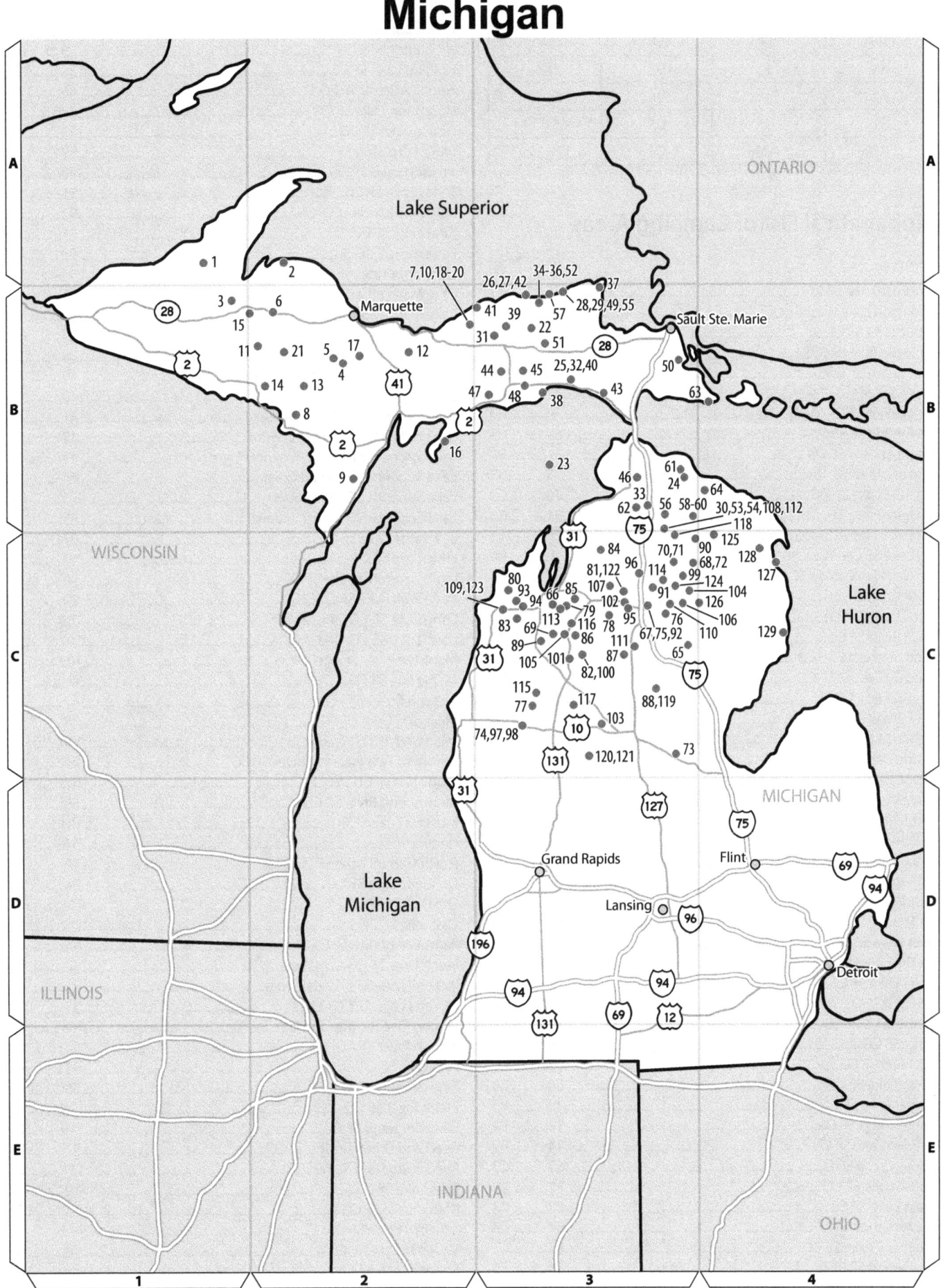

Map	ID	Map	ID
A1	1	B3	22-62
A2	2	B4	63-64
B1	3	C3	65-124
B2	4-21	C4	125-129

Alphabetical List of Camping Areas

Name	ID	Map
Ambrose Lake SF CG	65	C3
Anderson Lake West SF CG	4	B2
Arbutus #4 SF CG	66	C3
Au Sable River SF CG	67	C3
Avery Lake SF CG	68	C3
Bass Lake SF CG - Luce	22	B3
Bass Lake SF CG - Marquette	5	B2
Baxter Bridge SF CG	69	C3
Beaufort Lake SF CG	6	B2
Beaver Island SF	23	B3
Big Bear Lake SF CG	70	C3
Big Bear Point SF	71	C3
Big Eric's Bridge SF CG	2	A2
Big Lake SF CG	3	B1
Big Oaks Equestrian SF CG	72	C3
Black Creek SF CG	73	C3
Black Lake SF CG	24	B3
Black River SF CG	25	B3
Blind Sucker #1 SF CG	26	B3
Blind Sucker #2 SF CG	27	B3
Bodi Lake SF CG	28	B3
Bray Creek SF CG	74	C3
Burton's Landing SF CG	75	C3
Canoe Harbor SF CG	76	C3
Canoe Lake SF CG	7	B2
Carney Lake SF CG	8	B2
Carrieville SF CG	77	C3
CCC Bridge SF CG	78	C3
Cedar River North SF CG	9	B2
Culhane Lake SF CG	29	B3
Cusino Lake SF CG	10	B2
De Tour SF CG	63	B4
Deer Lake SF CG	11	B2
Elk Hill Equestrian SF CG	30	B3
Emily Lake SF CG	1	A1
Ess Lake SF CG	125	C4
Forest Lake SF CG	12	B2
Forks SF CG	79	C3
Fox River SF CG	31	B3
Garey Lake SF CG	80	C3
Garnet Lake SF CG	32	B3
Gene's Pond SF CG	13	B2
Glidden Lake SF CG	14	B2
Goose Creek SF CG	81	C3
Goose Lake SF CG	82	C3
Grass Lake SF CG	83	C3
Graves Crossing SF CG	84	C3
Guernsey Lake SF CG	85	C3
Haakwood SF CG	33	B3
Headquarters Lake Equestrian SF CG	34	B3
High Bridge SF CG	35	B3
Holland Lake SF CG	36	B3
Hopkins Creek SF CG	86	C3
Houghton Lake SF CG	87	C3
House Lake SF CG	88	C3
Indian Crossing SF CG	89	C3
Jackson Lake SF CG	90	C3
Jones Lake SF CG	91	C3
Keystone Landing SF CG	92	C3
King Lake SF CG	15	B2
Lake Ann SF CG	93	C3
Lake Dubonnet SF CG	94	C3
Lake Margrethe SF CG	95	C3
Lake Marjory SF CG	96	C3
Lake Superior SF - Andrus Lake	37	B3
Lake Superior SF - Big Knob	38	B3
Lake Superior SF - East Branch of Fox River	39	B3
Lake Superior SF - Hog Island	40	B3
Lake Superior SF - Kingston Lake	41	B3
Lake Superior SF - Lake Superior	42	B3
Lake Superior SF - Little Brevoort Lake North	43	B3
Lake Superior SF - Mead Creek	44	B3
Lake Superior SF - Portage Bay	16	B2
Lake Superior SF - South Manistique	45	B3
Leverentz Lake SF CG	97	C3
Little Lake SF CG	17	B2
LIttle Leverentz Lake SF CG	98	C3
Little Wolf Lake SF CG	99	C3
Long Lake SF CG - Missaukee	100	C3
Long Lake SF CG - Wexford	101	C3
Manistee River Bridge SF CG	102	C3
Maple Bay SF CG	46	B3
Merwin Creek SF CG	47	B3
Milakokia Lake SF CG	48	B3
Mio Pond SF CG	126	C4
Mouth of Two-Hearted River SF CG	49	B3
Mud Lake SF CG	103	C3
Munuscong River SF CG	50	B3
Muskrat Lake SF CG	104	C3
Natalie SF CG	51	B3
North Gemini Lake SF CG	18	B2
Ocqueoc Falls SF CG	64	B4
Old US 131 SF CG	105	C3
Ossineke SF CG	127	C4
Parmalee Bridge SF CG	106	C3
Perch Lake SF CG	52	B3
Pickerel Lake SF CG - Kalkaska	107	C3
Pickerel Lake SF CG - Otsego	53	B3
Pigeon River Bridge SF CG	108	C3
Pigeon River SF CG	54	B3
Pike Lake SF CG - Luce	55	B3
Pine Grove SF CG	56	B3
Platte River SF CG	109	C3
Rainbow Bend SF CG	110	C3
Reed and Green Bridge SF CG	57	B3
Reedsburg Dam SF CG	111	C3
Ross Lake SF CG	19	B2
Round Lake SF CG	112	C3
Scheck's Place SF CG	113	C3
Shoepac Lake SF CG	58	B3
Shupac Lake SF CG	114	C3

Campground	Page	Grid
Silver Creek SF CG	115	C3
South Gemini Lake SF CG	20	B2
Spring Lake SF CG	116	C3
Squaw Lake SF CG	21	B2
Sunrise Lake SF CG	117	C3
Thunder Bay River SF CG	128	C4
Tomahawk Creek Flooding SF CG	59	B3
Tomahawk Lake SF CG	60	B3
Town Corner SF CG	118	C3
Trout Lake SF CG	119	C3
Tubbs Lake Island SF CG	120	C3
Tubbs Lake Mainland SF CG	121	C3
Twin Lake SF CG	61	B3
Upper Manistee River SF CG	122	C3
Van Etten Lake SF CG	129	C4
Veterans Memorial SF CG	123	C3
Walsh Road SF CG - Equestrian	124	C3
Weber Lake SF CG	62	B3

1 • A1 | Emily Lake SF CG

Total sites: 9, RV sites: 9, Central water, Vault/pit toilet, No showers, No RV dump, Tent & RV camping: $20, MI Recreation Passport required -non-residents: $9/day or $34/annual/residents: $12-$17/annual, Open May-Oct, Max Length: 20ft, Reservations not accepted, Elev: 1217ft/371m, Tel: 906-288-3321, Nearest town: Houghton. GPS: 46.856715, -88.856604

2 • A2 | Big Eric's Bridge SF CG

Total sites: 21, RV sites: 21, Central water, Vault/pit toilet, No showers, No RV dump, Tent & RV camping: $20, MI Recreation Passport required -non-residents: $9/day or $34/annual/residents: $12-$17/annual, Open Apr-Nov, Max Length: 20ft, Reservations not accepted, Elev: 722ft/220m, Tel: 906-353-6558, Nearest town: L'Anse. GPS: 46.864809, -88.083646

3 • B1 | Big Lake SF CG

Total sites: 15, RV sites: 15, Central water, Vault/pit toilet, No showers, No RV dump, Tent & RV camping: $20, MI Recreation Passport required -non-residents: $9/day or $34/annual/residents: $12-$17/annual, Open May-Oct, Max Length: 20ft, Reservations not accepted, Elev: 1263ft/385m, Tel: 906-353-6558, Nearest town: Big Lake. GPS: 46.611676, -88.571937

4 • B2 | Anderson Lake West SF CG

Total sites: 13, RV sites: 13, Central water, Vault/pit toilet, No showers, No RV dump, Tent & RV camping: $20, MI Recreation Passport required -non-residents: $9/day or $34/annual/residents: $12-$17/annual, Open all year, Max Length: 40ft, Reservations not accepted, Elev: 1129ft/344m, Tel: 906-789-8217, Nearest town: Gwinn. GPS: 46.221869, -87.494898

5 • B2 | Bass Lake SF CG - Marquette

Total sites: 22, RV sites: 22, Central water, Vault/pit toilet, No showers, No RV dump, Tent & RV camping: $20, MI Recreation Passport required -non-residents: $9/day or $34/annual/residents: $12-$17/annual, Open all year, Max Length: 40ft, Reservations not accepted, Elev: 1227ft/374m, Tel: 906-786-2351, Nearest town: Gwinn. GPS: 46.263143, -87.586646

6 • B2 | Beaufort Lake SF CG

Total sites: 7, RV sites: 7, Central water, Vault/pit toilet, No showers, No RV dump, Tent & RV camping: $20, MI Recreation Passport required -non-residents: $9/day or $34/annual/residents: $12-$17/annual, Open May-Oct, Max Length: 20ft, Reservations not accepted, Elev: 1618ft/493m, Tel: 906-339-4461, Nearest town: Three Lakes. GPS: 46.547079, -88.187217

7 • B2 | Canoe Lake SF CG

Total sites: 4, RV sites: 4, Central water, Vault/pit toilet, No showers, No RV dump, Tent & RV camping: $20, MI Recreation Passport required -non-residents: $9/day or $34/annual/residents: $12-$17/annual, Open all year, Max Length: 20ft, Reservations not accepted, Elev: 882ft/269m, Tel: 906-341-2355, Nearest town: Munising. GPS: 46.458679, -86.291031

8 • B2 | Carney Lake SF CG

Total sites: 16, RV sites: 16, Central water, Vault/pit toilet, No showers, No RV dump, Tent & RV camping: $20, MI Recreation Passport required -non-residents: $9/day or $34/annual/residents: $12-$17/annual, Open May-Oct, Max Length: 40ft, Reservations not accepted, Elev: 1102ft/336m, Tel: 906-875-3324, Nearest town: Iron Mountain. GPS: 45.892583, -87.940901

9 • B2 | Cedar River North SF CG

Total sites: 18, RV sites: 14, Central water, Vault/pit toilet, No showers, No RV dump, Tent & RV camping: $20, MI Recreation Passport required -non-residents: $9/day or $34/annual/residents: $12-$17/annual, Open all year, Reservations not accepted, Elev: 659ft/201m, Tel: 906-863-9747, Nearest town: Cedar River. GPS: 45.499877, -87.390379

10 • B2 | Cusino Lake SF CG

Total sites: 6, RV sites: 6, Central water, Vault/pit toilet, No showers, No RV dump, Tent & RV camping: $20, MI Recreation Passport required -non-residents: $9/day or $34/annual/residents: $12-$17/annual, Open all year, Max Length: 20ft, Reservations not accepted, Elev: 860ft/262m, Tel: 906-341-2355, Nearest town: Melstrand. GPS: 46.450361, -86.260705

11 • B2 | Deer Lake SF CG

Total sites: 12, RV sites: 12, Central water, Vault/pit toilet, No showers, No RV dump, Tent & RV camping: $20, Season weather dependent, MI Recreation Passport required -non-residents: $9/day or $34/annual/residents: $12-$17/annual, Max Length: 20ft, Reservations not accepted, Elev: 1594ft/486m, Tel: 906-353-6558, Nearest town: Crystal Falls. GPS: 46.326203, -88.323969

12 • B2 | Forest Lake SF CG

Total sites: 26, RV sites: 26, Central water, Vault/pit toilet, No showers, No RV dump, Tent & RV camping: $20, MI Recreation Passport required -non-residents: $9/day or $34/annual/residents: $12-$17/annual, Open all year, Max Length: 40ft, Reservations not accepted, Elev: 786ft/240m, Tel: 906-341-2355, Nearest town: Chatham. GPS: 46.305335, -86.868762

13 • B2 | Gene's Pond SF CG

Total sites: 14, RV sites: 14, Central water, Vault/pit toilet, No showers, No RV dump, Tent & RV camping: $20, MI Recreation Passport required -non-residents: $9/day or $34/annual/residents:

$12-$17/annual, Open all year, Max Length: 20ft, Reservations not accepted, Elev: 1207ft/368m, Tel: 906-786-2351, Nearest town: Theodore. GPS: 46.072615, -87.865873

14 • B2 | Glidden Lake SF CG

Total sites: 23, RV sites: 23, Central water, Vault/pit toilet, No showers, No RV dump, Tent & RV camping: $20, MI Recreation Passport required -non-residents: $9/day or $34/annual/residents: $12-$17/annual, Open May-Oct, Max Length: 20ft, Reservations not accepted, Elev: 1365ft/416m, Tel: 906-875-3324, Nearest town: Crystal Falls. GPS: 46.070405, -88.237711

15 • B2 | King Lake SF CG

Total sites: 6, RV sites: 6, Central water, Vault/pit toilet, No showers, No RV dump, Tent & RV camping: $15, MI Recreation Passport required -non-residents: $9/day or $34/annual/residents: $12-$17/annual, Max Length: 20ft, Reservations not accepted, Elev: 1670ft/509m, Tel: 906-353-6558, Nearest town: L'Anse. GPS: 46.530941, -88.402747

16 • B2 | Lake Superior SF - Portage Bay

Total sites: 23, RV sites: 23, Central water, Vault/pit toilet, No showers, No RV dump, Tent & RV camping: $20, MI Recreation Passport required -non-residents: $9/day or $34/annual/residents: $12-$17/annual, Open all year, Max Length: 20ft, Reservations not accepted, Elev: 600ft/183m, Tel: 906-644-2603, Nearest town: Garden. GPS: 45.726683, -86.535501

17 • B2 | Little Lake SF CG

Total sites: 16, RV sites: 16, Central water, Vault/pit toilet, No showers, No RV dump, Tent & RV camping: $20, MI Recreation Passport required -non-residents: $9/day or $34/annual/residents: $12-$17/annual, Open all year, Max Length: 40ft, Reservations not accepted, Elev: 1125ft/343m, Tel: 906-786-2351, Nearest town: Gwinn. GPS: 46.281758, -87.333445

18 • B2 | North Gemini Lake SF CG

Total sites: 17, RV sites: 17, Central water, Vault/pit toilet, No showers, No RV dump, Tent & RV camping: $20, MI Recreation Passport required -non-residents: $9/day or $34/annual/residents: $12-$17/annual, Max Length: 20ft, Reservations not accepted, Elev: 925ft/282m, Tel: 906-341-2355, Nearest town: Melstrand. GPS: 46.490591, -86.305007

19 • B2 | Ross Lake SF CG

Total sites: 10, RV sites: 10, Central water, Vault/pit toilet, No showers, No RV dump, Tent & RV camping: $20, MI Recreation Passport required -non-residents: $9/day or $34/annual/residents: $12-$17/annual, Open all year, Max Length: 20ft, Reservations not accepted, Elev: 896ft/273m, Tel: 906-341-2355, Nearest town: Melstrand . GPS: 46.486955, -86.262166

20 • B2 | South Gemini Lake SF CG

Total sites: 8, RV sites: 8, Central water, Vault/pit toilet, No showers, No RV dump, Tent & RV camping: $15, MI Recreation Passport required -non-residents: $9/day or $34/annual/residents: $12-$17/annual, Max Length: 20ft, Reservations not accepted, Elev: 912ft/278m, Tel: 906-341-2355, Nearest town: Melstrand. GPS: 46.481752, -86.303319

21 • B2 | Squaw Lake SF CG

Total sites: 15, RV sites: 15, Central water, Vault/pit toilet, No showers, No RV dump, Tent & RV camping: $20, MI Recreation Passport required -non-residents: $9/day or $34/annual/residents: $12-$17/annual, Open May-Oct, Max Length: 40ft, Reservations not accepted, Elev: 1506ft/459m, Tel: 906-875-3324, Nearest town: Witch Lake. GPS: 46.291541, -88.061208

22 • B3 | Bass Lake SF CG - Luce

Total sites: 18, RV sites: 18, Central water, Vault/pit toilet, No showers, No RV dump, Tent & RV camping: $20, MI Recreation Passport required -non-residents: $9/day or $34/annual/residents: $12-$17/annual, Open all year, Max Length: 20ft, Reservations not accepted, Elev: 928ft/283m, Tel: 906-492-3415, Nearest town: Newberry. GPS: 46.462326, -85.708434

23 • B3 | Beaver Island SF

Total sites: 22, RV sites: 15, Central water, Vault/pit toilet, No showers, No RV dump, Tent & RV camping: $10, Ferry, MI Recreation Passport required -non-residents: $9/day or $34/annual/residents: $12-$17/annual, Open Apr-Oct, Max Length: 20ft, Reservations not accepted, Elev: 623ft/190m, Tel: 989-732-3541, Nearest town: St James. GPS: 45.582551, -85.537498

24 • B3 | Black Lake SF CG

Total sites: 52, RV sites: 52, Central water, Vault/pit toilet, No showers, No RV dump, Tent & RV camping: $20, MI Recreation Passport required -non-residents: $9/day or $34/annual/residents: $12-$17/annual, Open Apr-Nov, Max Length: 20ft, Reservations not accepted, Elev: 682ft/208m, Tel: 231-627-2811, Nearest town: Atlanta. GPS: 45.488259, -84.258667

25 • B3 | Black River SF CG

Total sites: 12, RV sites: 12, Central water, Vault/pit toilet, No showers, No RV dump, Tent & RV camping: $20, MI Recreation Passport required -non-residents: $9/day or $34/annual/residents: $12-$17/annual, Open all year, Max Length: 40ft, Reservations not accepted, Elev: 663ft/202m, Tel: 906-643-8620, Nearest town: Naubinway. GPS: 46.115553, -85.365934

26 • B3 | Blind Sucker #1 SF CG

Total sites: 17, RV sites: 17, Central water, Vault/pit toilet, No showers, No RV dump, Tent & RV camping: $20, MI Recreation Passport required -non-residents: $9/day or $34/annual/residents: $12-$17/annual, Open all year, Max Length: 20ft, Reservations not accepted, Elev: 643ft/196m, Tel: 906-658-3338, Nearest town: Newberry. GPS: 46.670092, -85.761628

27 • B3 | Blind Sucker #2 SF CG

Total sites: 31, RV sites: 31, Central water, Vault/pit toilet, No showers, No RV dump, Tent & RV camping: $20, MI Recreation Passport required -non-residents: $9/day or $34/annual/residents: $12-$17/annual, Open all year, Max Length: 20ft, Reservations not accepted, Elev: 646ft/197m, Tel: 906-658-3338, Nearest town: Deer Park. GPS: 46.666516, -85.752074

28 • B3 | Bodi Lake SF CG

Total sites: 12, RV sites: 12, Central water, Vault/pit toilet, No showers, No RV dump, Tent & RV camping: $20, MI Recreation Passport required -non-residents: $9/day or $34/annual/residents:

$12-$17/annual, Open all year, Max Length: 20ft, Reservations not accepted, Elev: 646ft/197m, Tel: 906-492-3415, Nearest town: Newberry. GPS: 46.704574, -85.337278

29 • B3 | Culhane Lake SF CG

Total sites: 15, RV sites: 15, Central water, Vault/pit toilet, No showers, No RV dump, Tent & RV camping: $20, MI Recreation Passport required -non-residents: $9/day or $34/annual/residents: $12-$17/annual, Open all year, Max Length: 20ft, Reservations not accepted, Elev: 633ft/193m, Tel: 906-492-3415, Nearest town: Newberry. GPS: 46.696902, -85.355523

30 • B3 | Elk Hill Equestrian SF CG

Total sites: 11, RV sites: 11, Central water, Vault/pit toilet, No showers, No RV dump, Tent & RV camping: $20, Group site: $6/person, MI Recreation Passport required -non-residents: $9/day or $34/annual/residents: $12-$17/annual, Open all year, Max Length: 40ft, Reservations accepted, Elev: 919ft/280m, Tel: 989-983-4101, Nearest town: Gaylord. GPS: 45.185302, -84.427236

31 • B3 | Fox River SF CG

Total sites: 7, RV sites: 7, Central water, Vault/pit toilet, No showers, No RV dump, Tent & RV camping: $20, MI Recreation Passport required -non-residents: $9/day or $34/annual/residents: $12-$17/annual, Open all year, Max Length: 20ft, Reservations not accepted, Elev: 774ft/236m, Tel: 906-341-2355, Nearest town: Seney. GPS: 46.407366, -86.045021

32 • B3 | Garnet Lake SF CG

Total sites: 10, RV sites: 10, Central water, Vault/pit toilet, No showers, No RV dump, Tent & RV camping: $15, MI Recreation Passport required -non-residents: $9/day or $34/annual/residents: $12-$17/annual, Max Length: 20ft, Reservations not accepted, Elev: 827ft/252m, Tel: 906-595-7202, Nearest town: Garnet. GPS: 46.154343, -85.294646

33 • B3 | Haakwood SF CG

Total sites: 18, RV sites: 18, Central water, Vault/pit toilet, No showers, No RV dump, Tent & RV camping: $20, MI Recreation Passport required -non-residents: $9/day or $34/annual/residents: $12-$17/annual, Open Apr-Nov, Reservations not accepted, Elev: 728ft/222m, Tel: 231-238-9392, Nearest town: Wolverine. GPS: 45.301667, -84.614722

34 • B3 | Headquarters Lake Equestrian SF CG

Total sites: 6, RV sites: 6, Central water, Vault/pit toilet, No showers, No RV dump, Tent & RV camping: $20, MI Recreation Passport required -non-residents: $9/day or $34/annual/residents: $12-$17/annual, Open all year, Reservations not accepted, Elev: 728ft/222m, Tel: 906-658-3338, Nearest town: Newberry. GPS: 46.624495, -85.603733

35 • B3 | High Bridge SF CG

Total sites: 6, RV sites: 6, Central water, Vault/pit toilet, No showers, No RV dump, Tent & RV camping: $20, MI Recreation Passport required -non-residents: $9/day or $34/annual/residents: $12-$17/annual, Open all year, Max Length: 20ft, Reservations not accepted, Elev: 745ft/227m, Tel: 906-658-3338, Nearest town: Newberry. GPS: 46.607465, -85.601752

36 • B3 | Holland Lake SF CG

Total sites: 15, RV sites: 15, Central water, Vault/pit toilet, No showers, No RV dump, Tent & RV camping: $20, MI Recreation Passport required -non-residents: $9/day or $34/annual/residents: $12-$17/annual, Open Apr-Oct, Max Length: 20ft, Reservations not accepted, Elev: 751ft/229m, Tel: 906-658-3338, Nearest town: Newberry. GPS: 46.615948, -85.656154

37 • B3 | Lake Superior SF - Andrus Lake

Total sites: 25, RV sites: 25, Central water, Vault/pit toilet, No showers, No RV dump, Tent & RV camping: $20, MI Recreation Passport required -non-residents: $9/day or $34/annual/residents: $12-$17/annual, Open all year, Max Length: 20ft, Reservations not accepted, Elev: 643ft/196m, Tel: 906-492-3415, Nearest town: Paradise. GPS: 46.703495, -85.037301

38 • B3 | Lake Superior SF - Big Knob

Total sites: 23, RV sites: 23, Central water, Vault/pit toilet, No showers, No RV dump, Tent & RV camping: $20, MI Recreation Passport required -non-residents: $9/day or $34/annual/residents: $12-$17/annual, Open all year, Max Length: 20ft, Reservations not accepted, Elev: 604ft/184m, Tel: 906-492-3415, Nearest town: Naubinway. GPS: 46.039074, -85.593825

39 • B3 | Lake Superior SF - East Branch of Fox River

Total sites: 19, RV sites: 19, Central water, Vault/pit toilet, No showers, No RV dump, Tent & RV camping: $20, MI Recreation Passport required -non-residents: $9/day or $34/annual/residents: $12-$17/annual, Open all year, Max Length: 20ft, Reservations not accepted, Elev: 840ft/256m, Tel: 906-341-2355, Nearest town: Seney. GPS: 46.465556, -85.945278

40 • B3 | Lake Superior SF - Hog Island

Total sites: 42, RV sites: 42, Central water, Vault/pit toilet, No showers, No RV dump, Tent & RV camping: $20, MI Recreation Passport required -non-residents: $9/day or $34/annual/residents: $12-$17/annual, Open all year, Max Length: 40ft, Reservations not accepted, Elev: 600ft/183m, Tel: 906-643-8620, Nearest town: Naubinway. GPS: 46.081450, -85.307170

41 • B3 | Lake Superior SF - Kingston Lake

Total sites: 16, RV sites: 16, Central water, Vault/pit toilet, No showers, No RV dump, Tent & RV camping: $20, MI Recreation Passport required -non-residents: $9/day or $34/annual/residents: $12-$17/annual, Open all year, Max Length: 40ft, Reservations not accepted, Elev: 820ft/250m, Tel: 906-341-2355, Nearest town: Munising. GPS: 46.585838, -86.226301

42 • B3 | Lake Superior SF - Lake Superior

Total sites: 18, RV sites: 18, Central water, Vault/pit toilet, No showers, No RV dump, Tent & RV camping: $20, MI Recreation Passport required -non-residents: $9/day or $34/annual/residents: $12-$17/annual, Open all year, Max Length: 20ft, Reservations not accepted, Elev: 612ft/187m, Tel: 906-658-3338, Nearest town: Grand Marais. GPS: 46.676951, -85.756797

43 • B3 | Lake Superior SF - Little Brevoort Lake North

Total sites: 20, RV sites: 20, Central water, Vault/pit toilet, No showers, No RV dump, Tent & RV camping: $20, MI Recreation Passport required -non-residents: $9/day or $34/annual/residents:

$12-$17/annual, Open all year, Max Length: 40ft, Reservations not accepted, Elev: 646ft/197m, Tel: 906-643-8620, Nearest town: Brevort. GPS: 46.019224, -85.016582

44 • B3 | Lake Superior SF - Mead Creek

Total sites: 9, RV sites: 9, Central water, Vault/pit toilet, No showers, No RV dump, Tent & RV camping: $20, MI Recreation Passport required -non-residents: $9/day or $34/annual/residents: $12-$17/annual, Open all year, Max Length: 20ft, Reservations not accepted, Elev: 650ft/198m, Tel: 906-341-2355, Nearest town: Germfask. GPS: 46.182581, -85.987108

45 • B3 | Lake Superior SF - South Manistique

Total sites: 29, RV sites: 29, Central water, Vault/pit toilet, No showers, No RV dump, Tent & RV camping: $20, MI Recreation Passport required -non-residents: $9/day or $34/annual/residents: $12-$17/annual, Open all year, Max Length: 40ft, Reservations not accepted, Elev: 689ft/210m, Tel: 906-293-5131, Nearest town: Manistique. GPS: 46.174431, -85.791184

46 • B3 | Maple Bay SF CG

Total sites: 35, RV sites: 35, Central water, Vault/pit toilet, No showers, No RV dump, Tent & RV camping: $20, MI Recreation Passport required -non-residents: $9/day or $34/annual/residents: $12-$17/annual, Open Apr-Nov, Max Length: 20ft, Reservations not accepted, Elev: 610ft/186m, Tel: 231-238-9392, Nearest town: Brutus. GPS: 45.487247, -84.707844

47 • B3 | Merwin Creek SF CG

Total sites: 10, RV sites: 10, Central water, Vault/pit toilet, No showers, No RV dump, Tent & RV camping: $20, MI Recreation Passport required -non-residents: $9/day or $34/annual/residents: $12-$17/annual, Max Length: 20ft, Reservations not accepted, Elev: 620ft/189m, Tel: 906-341-3618, Nearest town: Gulliver. GPS: 46.032472, -86.121882

48 • B3 | Milakokia Lake SF CG

Total sites: 35, RV sites: 35, Central water, Vault/pit toilet, No showers, No RV dump, Tent & RV camping: $20, MI Recreation Passport required -non-residents: $9/day or $34/annual/residents: $12-$17/annual, Open all year, Max Length: 40ft, Reservations not accepted, Elev: 738ft/225m, Tel: 906-293-5131, Nearest town: Naubinway. GPS: 46.083285, -85.791061

49 • B3 | Mouth of Two-Hearted River SF CG

Total sites: 36, RV sites: 36, Central water, Vault/pit toilet, No showers, No RV dump, Tent & RV camping: $20, MI Recreation Passport required -non-residents: $9/day or $34/annual/residents: $12-$17/annual, Max Length: 20ft, Reservations not accepted, Elev: 591ft/180m, Tel: 906-492-3415, Nearest town: Deer Park. GPS: 46.698072, -85.421661

50 • B3 | Munuscong River SF CG

Total sites: 25, RV sites: 25, Central water, Vault/pit toilet, No showers, No RV dump, Tent & RV camping: $20, MI Recreation Passport required -non-residents: $9/day or $34/annual/residents: $12-$17/annual, Open May-Nov, Reservations not accepted, Elev: 587ft/179m, Tel: 906-248-3422, Nearest town: Pickford. GPS: 46.226299, -84.279922

51 • B3 | Natalie SF CG

Total sites: 12, RV sites: 12, Central water, Vault/pit toilet, No showers, No RV dump, Tent & RV camping: $20, MI Recreation Passport required -non-residents: $9/day or $34/annual/residents: $12-$17/annual, Open all year, Max Length: 20ft, Reservations not accepted, Elev: 699ft/213m, Tel: 906-293-5131, Nearest town: Newberry. GPS: 46.350869, -85.579211

52 • B3 | Perch Lake SF CG

Total sites: 32, RV sites: 32, Central water, Vault/pit toilet, No showers, No RV dump, Tent & RV camping: $20, MI Recreation Passport required -non-residents: $9/day or $34/annual/residents: $12-$17/annual, Open all year, Max Length: 20ft, Reservations accepted, Elev: 679ft/207m, Tel: 906-658-3338, Nearest town: Newberry. GPS: 46.629416, -85.601705

53 • B3 | Pickerel Lake SF CG - Otsego

Total sites: 39, RV sites: 39, Central water, Vault/pit toilet, No showers, No RV dump, Tent & RV camping: $20, MI Recreation Passport required -non-residents: $9/day or $34/annual/residents: $12-$17/annual, Open all year, Reservations not accepted, Elev: 951ft/290m, Tel: 989-983-4101, Nearest town: Vanderbilt. GPS: 45.177422, -84.517618

54 • B3 | Pigeon River SF CG

Total sites: 19, RV sites: 19, Central water, Vault/pit toilet, No showers, No RV dump, Tent & RV camping: $20, MI Recreation Passport required -non-residents: $9/day or $34/annual/residents: $12-$17/annual, Open all year, Max Length: 20ft, Reservations not accepted, Elev: 912ft/278m, Tel: 989-732-5485, Nearest town: Gaylord. GPS: 45.176663, -84.428907

55 • B3 | Pike Lake SF CG - Luce

Total sites: 8, RV sites: 8, Central water, Vault/pit toilet, No showers, No RV dump, Tent & RV camping: $20, MI Recreation Passport required -non-residents: $9/day or $34/annual/residents: $12-$17/annual, Open Apr-Oct, Max Length: 20ft, Reservations not accepted, Elev: 712ft/217m, Tel: 906-492-3415, Nearest town: Gwinn. GPS: 46.644871, -85.411735

56 • B3 | Pine Grove SF CG

Total sites: 6, RV sites: 6, Central water, Vault/pit toilet, No showers, No RV dump, Tent & RV camping: $20, MI Recreation Passport required -non-residents: $9/day or $34/annual/residents: $12-$17/annual, Open all year, Max Length: 20ft, Reservations not accepted, Elev: 843ft/257m, Tel: 989-732-5485, Nearest town: Onoway. GPS: 45.244679, -84.446279

57 • B3 | Reed and Green Bridge SF CG

Total sites: 7, RV sites: 7, Central water, Vault/pit toilet, No showers, No RV dump, Tent & RV camping: $20, MI Recreation Passport required -non-residents: $9/day or $34/annual/residents: $12-$17/annual, Max Length: 20ft, Reservations not accepted, Elev: 646ft/197m, Tel: 906-492-3415, Nearest town: Newberry. GPS: 46.661457, -85.521899

58 • B3 | Shoepac Lake SF CG

Total sites: 25, RV sites: 25, Central water, Vault/pit toilet, No showers, No RV dump, Tent & RV camping: $20, MI Recreation Passport required -non-residents: $9/day or $34/annual/residents:

$12-$17/annual, Open Apr-Oct, Max Length: 20ft, Reservations not accepted, Elev: 863ft/263m, Tel: 231-625-2522, Nearest town: Onaway. GPS: 45.239941, -84.171163

59 • B3 | Tomahawk Creek Flooding SF CG

Total sites: 47, RV sites: 47, Central water, Vault/pit toilet, No showers, No RV dump, Tent & RV camping: $20, MI Recreation Passport required -non-residents: $9/day or $34/annual/residents: $12-$17/annual, Open Apr-Nov, Max Length: 30ft, Reservations not accepted, Elev: 866ft/264m, Tel: 231-625-2522, Nearest town: Onaway. GPS: 45.218804, -84.176734

60 • B3 | Tomahawk Lake SF CG

Total sites: 25, RV sites: 25, Central water, Vault/pit toilet, No showers, No RV dump, Tent & RV camping: $20, MI Recreation Passport required -non-residents: $9/day or $34/annual/residents: $12-$17/annual, Open Apr-Nov, Max Length: 20ft, Reservations not accepted, Elev: 820ft/250m, Tel: 231-625-2522, Nearest town: Onaway. GPS: 45.228085, -84.161465

61 • B3 | Twin Lake SF CG

Total sites: 11, RV sites: 11, Central water, Vault/pit toilet, No showers, No RV dump, Tent & RV camping: $20, MI Recreation Passport required -non-residents: $9/day or $34/annual/residents: $12-$17/annual, Open May-Sep, Max Length: 30ft, Reservations not accepted, Elev: 692ft/211m, Tel: 231-627-2811. GPS: 45.535702, -84.288946

62 • B3 | Weber Lake SF CG

Total sites: 18, RV sites: 18, Central water, Vault/pit toilet, No showers, No RV dump, Tent & RV camping: $20, MI Recreation Passport required -non-residents: $9/day or $34/annual/residents: $12-$17/annual, Open Apr-Nov, Max Length: 20ft, Reservations not accepted, Elev: 922ft/281m, Tel: 231-238-9392, Nearest town: Wolverine. GPS: 45.296552, -84.721808

63 • B4 | De Tour SF CG

Total sites: 21, RV sites: 21, Central water, Vault/pit toilet, No showers, No RV dump, Tent & RV camping: $20, MI Recreation Passport required -non-residents: $9/day or $34/annual/residents: $12-$17/annual, Open May-Oct, Reservations not accepted, Elev: 591ft/180m, Tel: 906-643-8620, Nearest town: De Tour. GPS: 45.957977, -84.000248

64 • B4 | Ocqueoc Falls SF CG

Total sites: 13, RV sites: 13, Central water, Vault/pit toilet, No showers, No RV dump, Tent & RV camping: $20, MI Recreation Passport required -non-residents: $9/day or $34/annual/residents: $12-$17/annual, Open May-Nov, Max Length: 20ft, Reservations not accepted, Elev: 715ft/218m, Tel: 989-734-2543, Nearest town: Rogers City. GPS: 45.394714, -84.056234

65 • C3 | Ambrose Lake SF CG

Total sites: 25, RV sites: 25, Central water, Vault/pit toilet, No showers, No RV dump, Tent & RV camping: $20, MI Recreation Passport required -non-residents: $9/day or $34/annual/residents: $12-$17/annual, Open all year, Reservations not accepted, Elev: 1293ft/394m, Tel: 989-473-2258, Nearest town: Rose City. GPS: 44.407512, -84.256427

66 • C3 | Arbutus #4 SF CG

Total sites: 25, RV sites: 25, Central water, Vault/pit toilet, No showers, No RV dump, Tent & RV camping: $20, MI Recreation Passport required -non-residents: $9/day or $34/annual/residents: $12-$17/annual, Open all year, Max Length: 20ft, Reservations not accepted, Elev: 814ft/248m, Tel: 231-922-5270, Nearest town: Traverse City. GPS: 44.673165, -85.522222

67 • C3 | Au Sable River SF CG

Total sites: 15, RV sites: 8, Central water, Vault/pit toilet, No showers, No RV dump, Tent & RV camping: $20, MI Recreation Passport required -non-residents: $9/day or $34/annual/residents: $12-$17/annual, Open all year, Max Length: 20ft, Reservations not accepted, Elev: 1125ft/343m, Tel: 989-348-7068, Nearest town: Grayling. GPS: 44.664074, -84.658988

68 • C3 | Avery Lake SF CG

Total sites: 16, RV sites: 13, Central water, Vault/pit toilet, No showers, No RV dump, Tent & RV camping: $20, MI Recreation Passport required -non-residents: $9/day or $34/annual/residents: $12-$17/annual, Open Apr-Nov, Max Length: 40ft, Reservations not accepted, Elev: 919ft/280m, Tel: 989-785-4388, Nearest town: Atlanta. GPS: 44.932203, -84.186916

69 • C3 | Baxter Bridge SF CG

Total sites: 25, RV sites: 25, Central water, Vault/pit toilet, No showers, No RV dump, Tent & RV camping: $20, MI Recreation Passport required -non-residents: $9/day or $34/annual/residents: $12-$17/annual, Open all year, Max Length: 40ft, Reservations not accepted, Elev: 896ft/273m, Tel: 231-775-7911, Nearest town: Manton. GPS: 44.493414, -85.522717

70 • C3 | Big Bear Lake SF CG

Total sites: 30, RV sites: 30, Central water, Vault/pit toilet, No showers, No RV dump, Tent & RV camping: $20, MI Recreation Passport required -non-residents: $9/day or $34/annual/residents: $12-$17/annual, Open Apr-Oct, Max Length: 20ft, Reservations accepted, Elev: 1289ft/393m, Tel: 989-732-5485, Nearest town: Vienna. GPS: 44.944477, -84.379996

71 • C3 | Big Bear Point SF

Total sites: 14, RV sites: 14, No water, Vault/pit toilet, Tent & RV camping: $20, MI Recreation Passport required -non-residents: $9/day or $34/annual/residents: $12-$17/annual, Open Apr-Oct, Reservations not accepted, Elev: 1237ft/377m, Tel: 989-732-5485, Nearest town: Gaylord. GPS: 44.942399, -84.386924

72 • C3 | Big Oaks Equestrian SF CG

Total sites: 24, RV sites: 24, Central water, Vault/pit toilet, No showers, No RV dump, Tent & RV camping: $20, User must provide generator for well pump, MI Recreation Passport required -non-residents: $9/day or $34/annual/residents: $12-$17/annual, Open Apr-Oct, Max Length: 40ft, Reservations not accepted, Elev: 945ft/288m, Tel: 989-785-4388, Nearest town: Atlanta. GPS: 44.926926, -84.191803

73 • C3 | Black Creek SF CG

Total sites: 23, RV sites: 23, Central water, Vault/pit toilet, No showers, No RV dump, Tent & RV camping: $20, MI Recreation Passport required -non-residents: $9/day or $34/annual/

residents: $12-$17/annual, Open May-Sep, Max Length: 40ft, Reservations not accepted, Elev: 676ft/206m, Tel: 989-386-4067. GPS: 43.710428, -84.397079

74 • C3 | Bray Creek SF CG

Total sites: 9, RV sites: 9, Central water, Vault/pit toilet, No showers, No RV dump, Tent & RV camping: $20, MI Recreation Passport required -non-residents: $9/day or $34/annual/residents: $12-$17/annual, Open all year, Max Length: 20ft, Reservations not accepted, Elev: 863ft/263m, Tel: 231-745-9465, Nearest town: Baldwin. GPS: 43.914413, -85.824115

75 • C3 | Burton's Landing SF CG

Total sites: 12, RV sites: 12, Central water, Vault/pit toilet, No showers, No RV dump, Tent & RV camping: $20, MI Recreation Passport required -non-residents: $9/day or $34/annual/residents: $12-$17/annual, Open all year, Max Length: 20ft, Reservations not accepted, Elev: 1119ft/341m, Tel: 989-348-7068, Nearest town: Grayling. GPS: 44.662705, -84.646753

76 • C3 | Canoe Harbor SF CG

Total sites: 45, RV sites: 45, Central water, Vault/pit toilet, No showers, No RV dump, Tent & RV camping: $20, MI Recreation Passport required -non-residents: $9/day or $34/annual/residents: $12-$17/annual, Open all year, Max Length: 20ft, Reservations not accepted, Elev: 1142ft/348m, Tel: 989-821-6125, Nearest town: Grayling. GPS: 44.607307, -84.469986

77 • C3 | Carrieville SF CG

Total sites: 31, RV sites: 31, Central water, Vault/pit toilet, No showers, No RV dump, Tent & RV camping: $20, MI Recreation Passport required -non-residents: $9/day or $34/annual/residents: $12-$17/annual, Open all year, Reservations not accepted, Elev: 968ft/295m, Tel: 231-745-9465, Nearest town: Luther. GPS: 44.036132, -85.723739

78 • C3 | CCC Bridge SF CG

Total sites: 32, RV sites: 32, Central water, Vault/pit toilet, No showers, No RV dump, Tent & RV camping: $20, MI Recreation Passport required -non-residents: $9/day or $34/annual/residents: $12-$17/annual, Open all year, Max Length: 20ft, Reservations not accepted, Elev: 1083ft/330m, Tel: 231-922-5270, Nearest town: Kalkaska. GPS: 44.613183, -84.992411

79 • C3 | Forks SF CG

Total sites: 9, RV sites: 9, Central water, Vault/pit toilet, No showers, No RV dump, Tent & RV camping: $20, MI Recreation Passport required -non-residents: $9/day or $34/annual/residents: $12-$17/annual, Open all year, Reservations not accepted, Elev: 866ft/264m, Tel: 231-922-5270, Nearest town: Williamsburg. GPS: 44.673214, -85.401376

80 • C3 | Garey Lake SF CG

Total sites: 12, RV sites: 12, Central water, Vault/pit toilet, No showers, No RV dump, Tent & RV camping: $20, MI Recreation Passport required -non-residents: $9/day or $34/annual/residents: $12-$17/annual, Open all year, Max Length: 20ft, Reservations not accepted, Elev: 856ft/261m, Tel: 231-276-9511, Nearest town: Empire. GPS: 44.777279, -85.938097

81 • C3 | Goose Creek SF CG

Total sites: 9, RV sites: 9, Central water, Vault/pit toilet, No showers, No RV dump, Tent & RV camping: $20, Equestrian group camp, MI Recreation Passport required -non-residents: $9/day or $34/annual/residents: $12-$17/annual, Open all year, Max Length: 20ft, Reservations not accepted, Elev: 1165ft/355m, Tel: 989-348-6371, Nearest town: Frederic. GPS: 44.761571, -84.839623

82 • C3 | Goose Lake SF CG

Total sites: 30, RV sites: 30, Central water, Vault/pit toilet, No showers, No RV dump, Tent & RV camping: $20, MI Recreation Passport required -non-residents: $9/day or $34/annual/residents: $12-$17/annual, Open all year, Max Length: 20ft, Reservations not accepted, Elev: 1302ft/397m, Tel: 231-775-7911, Nearest town: Lake City. GPS: 44.356723, -85.242994

83 • C3 | Grass Lake SF CG

Total sites: 15, RV sites: 15, Central water, Vault/pit toilet, No showers, No RV dump, Tent & RV camping: $20, MI Recreation Passport required -non-residents: $9/day or $34/annual/residents: $12-$17/annual, Max Length: 20ft, Reservations not accepted, Elev: 840ft/256m, Tel: 231-378-2144, Nearest town: Thompsonville. GPS: 44.592724, -85.848396

84 • C3 | Graves Crossing SF CG

Total sites: 10, RV sites: 10, Central water, Vault/pit toilet, No showers, No RV dump, Tent & RV camping: $20, MI Recreation Passport required -non-residents: $9/day or $34/annual/residents: $12-$17/annual, Open all year, Max Length: 20ft, Reservations not accepted, Elev: 774ft/236m, Tel: 231-582-7523, Nearest town: Mancelona. GPS: 45.023524, -85.056881

85 • C3 | Guernsey Lake SF CG

Total sites: 35, RV sites: 30, Central water, Vault/pit toilet, No showers, No RV dump, Tent & RV camping: $20, MI Recreation Passport required -non-residents: $9/day or $34/annual/residents: $12-$17/annual, Open all year, Max Length: 20ft, Reservations not accepted, Elev: 974ft/297m, Tel: 231-922-5270, Nearest town: Kalkaska. GPS: 44.715755, -85.322958

86 • C3 | Hopkins Creek SF CG

Total sites: 7, RV sites: 7, Central water, Vault/pit toilet, No showers, No RV dump, Tent & RV camping: $20, MI Recreation Passport required -non-residents: $9/day or $34/annual/residents: $12-$17/annual, Open all year, Max Length: 20ft, Reservations not accepted, Elev: 1047ft/319m, Tel: 231-775-7911, Nearest town: Arlene. GPS: 44.482187, -85.321286

87 • C3 | Houghton Lake SF CG

Total sites: 50, RV sites: 50, Central water, Vault/pit toilet, No showers, No RV dump, Tent & RV camping: $20, MI Recreation Passport required -non-residents: $9/day or $34/annual/residents: $12-$17/annual, Open Apr-Sep, Max Length: 40ft, Reservations not accepted, Elev: 1152ft/351m, Tel: 989-821-6125, Nearest town: Houghton Lake. GPS: 44.401199, -84.771045

88 • C3 | House Lake SF CG

Total sites: 41, RV sites: 41, Central water, Vault/pit toilet, No showers, No RV dump, Tent & RV camping: $20, MI Recreation Passport required -non-residents: $9/day or $34/annual/residents:

$12-$17/annual, Open all year, Max Length: 40ft, Reservations not accepted, Elev: 1053ft/321m, Tel: 989-386-4067, Nearest town: Harrison. GPS: 44.140509, -84.572145

89 • C3 | Indian Crossing SF CG

Dispersed sites, No water, No toilets, Tent & RV camping: Fee unk, MI Recreation Passport required -non-residents: $9/day or $34/annual/residents: $12-$17/annual, Elev: 852ft/260m, Nearest town: Mesick. GPS: 44.451293, -85.633899

90 • C3 | Jackson Lake SF CG

Total sites: 18, RV sites: 15, Central water, Vault/pit toilet, No showers, No RV dump, Tent & RV camping: $20, MI Recreation Passport required -non-residents: $9/day or $34/annual/residents: $12-$17/annual, Open Apr-Nov, Max Length: 40ft, Reservations not accepted, Elev: 909ft/277m, Tel: 989-785-4388, Nearest town: Atlanta. GPS: 45.088982, -84.160752

91 • C3 | Jones Lake SF CG

Total sites: 42, RV sites: 42, Central water, Vault/pit toilet, No showers, No RV dump, Tent & RV camping: $20, MI Recreation Passport required -non-residents: $9/day or $34/annual/residents: $12-$17/annual, Open all year, Max Length: 20ft, Reservations not accepted, Elev: 1217ft/371m, Tel: 989-348-7068, Nearest town: Grayling. GPS: 44.784346, -84.589032

92 • C3 | Keystone Landing SF CG

Total sites: 18, RV sites: 18, Central water, Vault/pit toilet, No showers, No RV dump, Tent & RV camping: $20, MI Recreation Passport required -non-residents: $9/day or $34/annual/residents: $12-$17/annual, Open all year, Max Length: 20ft, Reservations not accepted, Elev: 1102ft/336m, Tel: 989-348-7068, Nearest town: Grayling. GPS: 44.665431, -84.624915

93 • C3 | Lake Ann SF CG

Total sites: 30, RV sites: 30, Central water, Vault/pit toilet, No showers, No RV dump, Tent & RV camping: $20, MI Recreation Passport required -non-residents: $9/day or $34/annual/residents: $12-$17/annual, Open all year, Max Length: 20ft, Reservations not accepted, Elev: 781ft/238m, Tel: 231-276-9511, Nearest town: Laingsburg. GPS: 44.712151, -85.860944

94 • C3 | Lake Dubonnet SF CG

Total sites: 50, RV sites: 50, Central water, Vault/pit toilet, No showers, No RV dump, Tent & RV camping: $20, MI Recreation Passport required -non-residents: $9/day or $34/annual/residents: $12-$17/annual, Open all year, Max Length: 20ft, Reservations not accepted, Elev: 882ft/269m, Tel: 231-276-9511, Nearest town: Interlochen. GPS: 44.671466, -85.798716

95 • C3 | Lake Margrethe SF CG

Total sites: 37, RV sites: 37, Central water, Vault/pit toilet, No showers, No RV dump, Tent & RV camping: $20, MI Recreation Passport required -non-residents: $9/day or $34/annual/residents: $12-$17/annual, Open May-Sep, Max Length: 20ft, Reservations accepted, Elev: 1135ft/346m, Tel: 989-348-7068, Nearest town: Grayling. GPS: 44.657928, -84.816968

96 • C3 | Lake Marjory SF CG

Total sites: 10, RV sites: 10, Central water, Vault/pit toilet, No showers, No RV dump, Tent & RV camping: $20, MI Recreation Passport required -non-residents: $9/day or $34/annual/residents: $12-$17/annual, Open Apr-Oct, Max Length: 40ft, Reservations not accepted, Elev: 1260ft/384m, Tel: 989-732-5485. GPS: 44.871215, -84.694857

97 • C3 | Leverentz Lake SF CG

Total sites: 18, RV sites: 18, Central water, Vault/pit toilet, No showers, No RV dump, Tent & RV camping: $20, MI Recreation Passport required -non-residents: $9/day or $34/annual/residents: $12-$17/annual, Max Length: 20ft, Reservations not accepted, Elev: 881ft/269m, Tel: 231-745-9465, Nearest town: Baldwin. GPS: 43.908742, -85.819465

98 • C3 | LIttle Leverentz Lake SF CG

Total sites: 7, RV sites: 7, Central water, Vault/pit toilet, No showers, No RV dump, Tent & RV camping: $15, MI Recreation Passport required -non-residents: $9/day or $34/annual/residents: $12-$17/annual, Open all year, Max Length: 20ft, Reservations not accepted, Elev: 889ft/271m, Tel: 231-745-9465, Nearest town: Baldwin. GPS: 43.906263, -85.822769

99 • C3 | Little Wolf Lake SF CG

Total sites: 24, RV sites: 24, Central water, Vault/pit toilet, No showers, No RV dump, Tent & RV camping: $20, MI Recreation Passport required -non-residents: $9/day or $34/annual/residents: $12-$17/annual, Open Apr-Oct, Max Length: 40ft, Reservations not accepted, Elev: 1220ft/372m, Tel: 989-732-5485. GPS: 44.855196, -84.286619

100 • C3 | Long Lake SF CG - Missaukee

Total sites: 11, RV sites: 11, Central water, Vault/pit toilet, No showers, No RV dump, Tent & RV camping: $20, MI Recreation Passport required -non-residents: $9/day or $34/annual/residents: $12-$17/annual, Open Apr-Oct, Max Length: 20ft, Reservations not accepted, Elev: 1270ft/387m, Tel: 231-775-7911, Nearest town: Lake City. GPS: 44.354865, -85.252607

101 • C3 | Long Lake SF CG - Wexford

Total sites: 12, RV sites: 12, Central water, Vault/pit toilet, No showers, No RV dump, Tent & RV camping: $20, MI Recreation Passport required -non-residents: $9/day or $34/annual/residents: $12-$17/annual, Open all year, Reservations not accepted, Elev: 1289ft/393m, Tel: 231-775-7911, Nearest town: Cadillac. GPS: 44.333544, -85.375324

102 • C3 | Manistee River Bridge SF CG

Total sites: 23, RV sites: 23, Central water, Vault/pit toilet, No showers, No RV dump, Tent & RV camping: $20, MI Recreation Passport required -non-residents: $9/day or $34/annual/residents: $12-$17/annual, Open all year, Max Length: 20ft, Reservations not accepted, Elev: 1145ft/349m, Tel: 989-348-7068, Nearest town: Grayling. GPS: 44.693609, -84.847594

103 • C3 | Mud Lake SF CG

Total sites: 8, RV sites: 8, Central water, Vault/pit toilet, No showers, No RV dump, Tent & RV camping: $20, MI Recreation Passport required -non-residents: $9/day or $34/annual/residents: $12-$17/annual, Open all year, Max Length: 20ft, Reservations not accepted, Elev: 1053ft/321m, Tel: 989-386-4067, Nearest town: Evart. GPS: 43.907446, -85.078806

104 • C3 | Muskrat Lake SF CG

Total sites: 13, RV sites: 13, Central water, Vault/pit toilet, No showers, No RV dump, Tent & RV camping: $20, MI Recreation Passport required -non-residents: $9/day or $34/annual/residents: $12-$17/annual, Open all year, Max Length: 40ft, Reservations not accepted, Elev: 1174ft/358m, Tel: 989-348-6371, Nearest town: Mio. GPS: 44.752537, -84.240355

105 • C3 | Old US 131 SF CG

Total sites: 25, RV sites: 25, Central water, Vault/pit toilet, No showers, No RV dump, Tent & RV camping: $20, MI Recreation Passport required -non-residents: $9/day or $34/annual/residents: $12-$17/annual, Open all year, Max Length: 20ft, Reservations not accepted, Elev: 958ft/292m, Tel: 231-775-7911, Nearest town: Manton. GPS: 44.491953, -85.417881

106 • C3 | Parmalee Bridge SF CG

Total sites: 7, RV sites: 7, Central water, Vault/pit toilet, No showers, No RV dump, Tent & RV camping: $20, Group site, MI Recreation Passport required -non-residents: $9/day or $34/annual/residents: $12-$17/annual, Open Apr-Nov, Max Length: 20ft, Reservations not accepted, Elev: 1024ft/312m, Tel: 989-473-2258, Nearest town: Mio. GPS: 44.677554, -84.292617

107 • C3 | Pickerel Lake SF CG - Kalkaska

Total sites: 13, RV sites: 13, Central water, Vault/pit toilet, No showers, No RV dump, Tent & RV camping: $20, MI Recreation Passport required -non-residents: $9/day or $34/annual/residents: $12-$17/annual, Open all year, Reservations not accepted, Elev: 1250ft/381m, Tel: 231-922-5280, Nearest town: Kalkaska. GPS: 44.796648, -84.973915

108 • C3 | Pigeon River Bridge SF CG

Total sites: 10, RV sites: 10, Central water, Vault/pit toilet, No showers, No RV dump, Tent & RV camping: $20, MI Recreation Passport required -non-residents: $9/day or $34/annual/residents: $12-$17/annual, Open Apr-Oct, Max Length: 20ft, Reservations not accepted, Elev: 942ft/287m, Tel: 989-732-5485, Nearest town: Gaylord. GPS: 45.156664, -84.465125

109 • C3 | Platte River SF CG

Total sites: 26, RV sites: 26, Central water, Vault/pit toilet, No showers, No RV dump, Tent & RV camping: $20, MI Recreation Passport required -non-residents: $9/day or $34/annual/residents: $12-$17/annual, Open all year, Reservations not accepted, Elev: 659ft/201m, Tel: 231-276-9511, Nearest town: Honor. GPS: 44.645177, -85.978313

110 • C3 | Rainbow Bend SF CG

Total sites: 7, RV sites: 7, Central water, Vault/pit toilet, No showers, No RV dump, Tent & RV camping: $20, MI Recreation Passport required -non-residents: $9/day or $34/annual/residents: $12-$17/annual, Open all year, Max Length: 20ft, Reservations not accepted, Elev: 1070ft/326m, Tel: 989-348-7068, Nearest town: Grayling. GPS: 44.670138, -84.417383

111 • C3 | Reedsburg Dam SF CG

Total sites: 47, RV sites: 47, Central water, Vault/pit toilet, No showers, No RV dump, Tent & RV camping: $20, MI Recreation Passport required -non-residents: $9/day or $34/annual/residents: $12-$17/annual, Open all year, Max Length: 40ft, Reservations not accepted, Elev: 1165ft/355m, Tel: 989-821-6125, Nearest town: Houghton Lake. GPS: 44.358475, -84.857937

112 • C3 | Round Lake SF CG

Total sites: 10, RV sites: 10, Central water, Vault/pit toilet, No showers, No RV dump, Tent & RV camping: $20, MI Recreation Passport required -non-residents: $9/day or $34/annual/residents: $12-$17/annual, Open all year, Max Length: 20ft, Reservations not accepted, Elev: 984ft/300m, Tel: 989-732-5485, Nearest town: Vanderbilt. GPS: 45.136188, -84.453023

113 • C3 | Scheck's Place SF CG

Total sites: 30, RV sites: 30, Central water, Vault/pit toilet, No showers, No RV dump, Tent & RV camping: $20, MI Recreation Passport required -non-residents: $9/day or $34/annual/residents: $12-$17/annual, Open all year, Max Length: 20ft, Reservations not accepted, Elev: 824ft/251m, Tel: 231-922-5270, Nearest town: Mayfield. GPS: 44.652537, -85.456631

114 • C3 | Shupac Lake SF CG

Total sites: 30, RV sites: 30, Central water, Vault/pit toilet, No showers, No RV dump, Tent & RV camping: $20, MI Recreation Passport required -non-residents: $9/day or $34/annual/residents: $12-$17/annual, Open all year, Reservations not accepted, Elev: 1188ft/362m, Tel: 989-348-7068, Nearest town: Lovells. GPS: 44.822261, -84.478925

115 • C3 | Silver Creek SF CG

Total sites: 26, RV sites: 26, Central water, Vault/pit toilet, No showers, No RV dump, Tent & RV camping: $20, MI Recreation Passport required -non-residents: $9/day or $34/annual/residents: $12-$17/annual, Open all year, Max Length: 20ft, Reservations not accepted, Elev: 958ft/292m, Tel: 231-745-9465, Nearest town: Luther. GPS: 44.118547, -85.684947

116 • C3 | Spring Lake SF CG

Total sites: 30, RV sites: 30, Central water, Vault/pit toilet, No showers, No RV dump, Tent & RV camping: $20, MI Recreation Passport required -non-residents: $9/day or $34/annual/residents: $12-$17/annual, Open all year, Max Length: 20ft, Reservations not accepted, Elev: 1030ft/314m, Tel: 231-775-7911, Nearest town: Traverse City. GPS: 44.563107, -85.362807

117 • C3 | Sunrise Lake SF CG

Total sites: 17, RV sites: 15, Central water, Vault/pit toilet, No showers, No RV dump, Tent & RV camping: $20, MI Recreation Passport required -non-residents: $9/day or $34/annual/residents: $12-$17/annual, Open all year, Max Length: 20ft, Elev: 1260ft/384m, Tel: 989-386-4067, Nearest town: LeRoy. GPS: 44.029247, -85.332716

118 • C3 | Town Corner SF CG

Total sites: 12, RV sites: 12, Central water, Vault/pit toilet, No showers, No RV dump, Tent & RV camping: $20, MI Recreation Passport required -non-residents: $9/day or $34/annual/residents:

$12-$17/annual, Open Apr-Oct, Max Length: 20ft, Reservations not accepted, Elev: 928ft/283m, Tel: 989-732-5485, Nearest town: Johannesburg. GPS: 45.115143, -84.361832

119 • C3 | Trout Lake SF CG

Total sites: 35, RV sites: 35, Central water, Vault/pit toilet, No showers, No RV dump, Tent & RV camping: $20, MI Recreation Passport required -non-residents: $9/day or $34/annual/residents: $12-$17/annual, Open all year, Max Length: 40ft, Reservations not accepted, Elev: 1030ft/314m, Tel: 989-386-4067, Nearest town: Meredith. GPS: 44.134207, -84.564402

120 • C3 | Tubbs Lake Island SF CG

Total sites: 12, RV sites: 12, No water, Vault/pit toilet, No showers, No RV dump, Tent & RV camping: $13, MI Recreation Passport required -non-residents: $9/day or $34/annual/residents: $12-$17/annual, Max Length: 30ft, Reservations not accepted, Elev: 1010ft/308m, Tel: 231-775-9727, Nearest town: Mecosta. GPS: 43.714011, -85.210239

121 • C3 | Tubbs Lake Mainland SF CG

Total sites: 21, RV sites: 21, Central water, Vault/pit toilet, No showers, No RV dump, Tent & RV camping: $13, MI Recreation Passport required -non-residents: $9/day or $34/annual/residents: $12-$17/annual, Max Length: 30ft, Reservations not accepted, Elev: 1004ft/306m, Tel: 231-775-9727, Nearest town: Mecosta. GPS: 43.711242, -85.198487

122 • C3 | Upper Manistee River SF CG

Total sites: 30, RV sites: 30, Central water, Vault/pit toilet, No showers, No RV dump, Tent & RV camping: $20, Group site, MI Recreation Passport required -non-residents: $9/day or $34/annual/residents: $12-$17/annual, Open all year, Max Length: 20ft, Reservations not accepted, Elev: 1142ft/348m, Tel: 989-348-7068. GPS: 44.750506, -84.839202

123 • C3 | Veterans Memorial SF CG

Total sites: 24, RV sites: 24, Central water, Vault/pit toilet, No showers, No RV dump, Tent & RV camping: $20, MI Recreation Passport required -non-residents: $9/day or $34/annual/residents: $12-$17/annual, Max Length: 20ft, Reservations not accepted, Elev: 692ft/211m, Tel: 231-276-9511, Nearest town: Honor. GPS: 44.658321, -85.945233

124 • C3 | Walsh Road SF CG - Equestrian

Total sites: 9, RV sites: 9, Central water, Vault/pit toilet, No showers, No RV dump, Tent & RV camping: $20, Group equestrian site, MI Recreation Passport required -non-residents: $9/day or $34/annual/residents: $12-$17/annual, Open all year, Max Length: 20ft, Reservations not accepted, Elev: 1171ft/357m, Tel: 989-348-7068, Nearest town: Grayling. GPS: 44.783463, -84.372294

125 • C4 | Ess Lake SF CG

Total sites: 27, RV sites: 27, Central water, Vault/pit toilet, No showers, No RV dump, Tent & RV camping: $20, MI Recreation Passport required -non-residents: $9/day or $34/annual/residents: $12-$17/annual, Open Apr-Nov, Max Length: 20ft, Reservations not accepted, Elev: 827ft/252m, Tel: 989-785-4388, Nearest town: Atlanta. GPS: 45.109534, -83.981471

126 • C4 | Mio Pond SF CG

Total sites: 24, RV sites: 24, Central water, Vault/pit toilet, No showers, No RV dump, Tent & RV camping: $15, MI Recreation Passport required -non-residents: $9/day or $34/annual/residents: $12-$17/annual, Open Apr-Nov, Max Length: 20ft, Reservations not accepted, Elev: 974ft/297m, Tel: 989-473-2258, Nearest town: Mio. GPS: 44.663466, -84.145979

127 • C4 | Ossineke SF CG

Total sites: 42, RV sites: 42, Central water, Vault/pit toilet, No showers, No RV dump, Tent & RV camping: $20, MI Recreation Passport required -non-residents: $9/day or $34/annual/residents: $12-$17/annual, Open all year, Max Length: 20ft, Reservations not accepted, Elev: 564ft/172m, Tel: 989-724-5126. GPS: 44.919896, -83.410399

128 • C4 | Thunder Bay River SF CG

Total sites: 10, RV sites: 10, Central water, Vault/pit toilet, No showers, No RV dump, Tent & RV camping: $20, MI Recreation Passport required -non-residents: $9/day or $34/annual/residents: $12-$17/annual, Open May-Nov, Max Length: 30ft, Reservations not accepted, Elev: 722ft/220m, Tel: 989-785-4251, Nearest town: Alpena. GPS: 45.015844, -83.557343

129 • C4 | Van Etten Lake SF CG

Total sites: 49, RV sites: 49, Central water, Vault/pit toilet, No showers, No RV dump, Tent & RV camping: $20, MI Recreation Passport required -non-residents: $9/day or $34/annual/residents: $12-$17/annual, Open May-Oct, Max Length: 40ft, Reservations not accepted, Elev: 591ft/180m, Tel: 989-362-5041, Nearest town: Oscoda. GPS: 44.470887, -83.369742

Minnesota

Map	ID	Map	ID
A1	1	C2	40-56
A2	2	C3	57-61
A3	3-5	D3	62-65
B2	6-19	E3	66-67
B3	20-33	E4	68
B4	34-39		

Alphabetical List of Camping Areas

Name	ID	Map
Beltrami Island SF - Bemis Hill	1	A1
Beltrami Island SF - Faunce	2	A2
Birch Lakes SF	40	C2
Bowstring SF - Cottonwood Lake	6	B2
Bowstring SF - Moose Lake	7	B2
Centennial SF - Dispersed 1	8	B2
Chengwatana SF - Snake River CG	57	C3
Cloquet Vallet SF - Indian Lake CG	20	B3
Cloquet Valley SF	21	B3
Cloquet Valley SF - Bear Lake	22	B3
Cloquet Valley SF - Cloquet River Water Camp	23	B3
Crow Wing SF - Greer Lake CG	41	C2
Finland SF - Eckbeck CG	34	B4
Finland SF - Finland CG	35	B4
Finland SF - Sullivan Lake	24	B3
Foothills SF	42	C2
FSR 2417 Dispersed 1	9	B2
Gen. G C Andrews SF - Button Box	25	B3
Gen. G C Andrews SF - Willow River	58	C3
Geo. Washington SF - Larson Lake	26	B3
Geo. Washington SF - Lost Lake	27	B3
Geo. Washington SF - Owen Lake	28	B3
Geo. Washington SF - Stony Brook Horse Camp	29	B3
Geo. Washington SF - Thistledew Lake CG	30	B3
Geo. Washington SF - Togo Horse	31	B3
Grand Portage SF - Devilfish Lake	36	B4
Grand Portage SF - Esther Lake	37	B4
Grand Portage SF - McFarland Lake	38	B4
Huntersville SF - Landing (77.7R)	43	C2
Huntersville SF - Shell City Horse Camp	44	C2
Huntersville SF - Shell City Landing	45	C2
Kabetogama SF - Ash River	3	A3
Kabetogama SF - Wakemup Bay CG	32	B3
Kabetogama SF - Woodenfrog CG	4	A3
Koochiching SF Dispersed 1	5	A3
Land O'Lakes SF - Clint Converse	10	B2
Land O'Lakes SF Dispersed 1	46	C2
Nemadji SF - Garfvert CG	59	C3
Pat Bayle SF - Twin Lakes	39	B4
Paul Bunyan SF - Gulch Lake	11	B2
Paul Bunyan SF - Mantrap Lake	12	B2
Paul Bunyan SF Dispersed 1	13	B2
Paul Bunyan SF Dispersed 2	14	B2
Paul Bunyan SF Dispersed 3	15	B2
Paul Bunyan SF Dispersed 4	16	B2
Paul Bunyan SF Dispersed 5	17	B2
Pillsbury SF - Rock Lake CG	47	C2
Pillsbury SF - Walter E Stark Horse Camp	48	C2
Red Lake SF - Waskish	18	B2
Richard J. Dorer SF - Kruger CG	62	D3
Richard J. Dorer SF - Money Creek/Vinegar Ridge	66	E3
Richard J. Dorer SF - Oak Ridge/Wet Bark	67	E3
Richard J. Dorer SF - Reno Horse Camp	68	E4
Richard J. Dorer SF - Zumbro Bottom Horse Camp Central	63	D3
Richard J. Dorer SF - Zumbro Bottom Horse Camp North	64	D3
Richard J. Dorer SF - Zumbro Bottom Horse Camp West	65	D3
Rum River SF - Esker Trail Dispersed	49	C2
Rum River SF - Game Refuge Rd	50	C2
Rum River SF - Kanabec Forest Rd Dispersed 1	51	C2
Rum River SF - Kanabec Forest Rd Dispersed 2	52	C2
Rum River SF - Riders Trail Dispersed	53	C2
Rum River SF - Unnamed Rd Dispersed 1	54	C2
Sand Dunes SF - Ann Lake	55	C2
Sand Dunes SF - Bob Dunn Horse Camp	56	C2
Savanna SF - Hay Lake	33	B3
St Croix SF - Boulder	60	C3
St Croix SF - Tamarack Horse Camp	61	C3
Two Inlets SF - Hungryman Lake	19	B2

1 • A1 | Beltrami Island SF - Bemis Hill

Total sites: 10, RV sites: 6, Central water, Vault/pit toilet, No showers, No RV dump, Tent & RV camping: $14-15, 4 horse sites, Reservations not accepted, Elev: 1266ft/386m, Tel: 218-425-7504, Nearest town: Roseau. GPS: 48.710851, -95.459755

2 • A2 | Beltrami Island SF - Faunce

Total sites: 6, RV sites: 6, Central water, Vault/pit toilet, Tent & RV camping: $14-15, Open Apr-Nov, Reservations not accepted, Elev: 1280ft/390m, Tel: 218-783-6252, Nearest town: Williams. GPS: 48.590921, -94.952445

3 • A3 | Kabetogama SF - Ash River

Total sites: 8, RV sites: 8, Central water, Vault/pit toilet, No showers, No RV dump, Tent & RV camping: $17, Reservations not accepted, Elev: 1184ft/361m, Tel: 218-365-7229, Nearest town: Orr. GPS: 48.406423, -92.813938

4 • A3 | Kabetogama SF - Woodenfrog CG

Total sites: 59, RV sites: 59, Central water, Vault/pit toilet, No showers, No RV dump, Tent & RV camping: $17, Reservations not accepted, Elev: 1125ft/343m, Tel: 218-365-7229, Nearest town: Kabetogama Lake. GPS: 48.481545, -93.065406

5 • A3 | Koochiching SF Dispersed 1

Dispersed sites, No water, No toilets, Tent & RV camping: Free, Elev: 1135ft/346m. GPS: 48.488387, -93.230394

6 • B2 | Bowstring SF - Cottonwood Lake

Total sites: 10, RV sites: 10, Central water, Vault/pit toilet, No showers, No RV dump, Tent & RV camping: $17, Reservations not accepted, Elev: 1342ft/409m, Tel: 218-743-3362, Nearest town: Calumet. GPS: 47.427682, -93.697866

7 • B2 | Bowstring SF - Moose Lake

Total sites: 11, RV sites: 11, Central water, Vault/pit toilet, No showers, No RV dump, Tent & RV camping: $17, Reservations not accepted, Elev: 1312ft/400m, Tel: 218-743-3362, Nearest town: Deer River. GPS: 47.399701, -93.712921

8 • B2 | Centennial SF - Dispersed 1

Dispersed sites, No water, No toilets, Tent & RV camping: Free, Reservations not accepted, Elev: 1366ft/416m, Nearest town: Longville. GPS: 46.909661, -94.126253

9 • B2 | FSR 2417 Dispersed 1

Dispersed sites, No water, No toilets, Tent & RV camping: Free, Stay limit: 14-21 days, Reservations not accepted, Elev: 1331ft/406m, Tel: 651-296-6157, Nearest town: Blackduck. GPS: 47.617783, -94.571627

10 • B2 | Land O'Lakes SF - Clint Converse

Total sites: 31, RV sites: 31, Central water, Vault/pit toilet, No showers, No RV dump, Tent & RV camping: $17, Open May-Oct, Reservations not accepted, Elev: 1326ft/404m, Tel: 218-546-5926, Nearest town: Ironton. GPS: 46.850058, -93.978391

11 • B2 | Paul Bunyan SF - Gulch Lake

Total sites: 8, RV sites: 8, Central water, Vault/pit toilet, No showers, No RV dump, Tent & RV camping: $17, Reservations not accepted, Elev: 1440ft/439m, Tel: 218-308-2300, Nearest town: Laporte. GPS: 47.160391, -94.836615

12 • B2 | Paul Bunyan SF - Mantrap Lake

Total sites: 38, RV sites: 36, Central water, Vault/pit toilet, No showers, No RV dump, Tent & RV camping: $17, Reservations not accepted, Elev: 1503ft/458m, Tel: 218-266-2100, Nearest town: Park Rapids. GPS: 47.066060, -94.936580

13 • B2 | Paul Bunyan SF Dispersed 1

Dispersed sites, No water, No toilets, Tent & RV camping: Free, Stay limit: 14-21 days, Reservations not accepted, Elev: 1558ft/475m, Tel: 651-296-6157, Nearest town: Laporte. GPS: 47.164164, -94.882467

14 • B2 | Paul Bunyan SF Dispersed 2

Dispersed sites, No water, No toilets, Tent & RV camping: Free, Stay limit: 14-21 days, Reservations not accepted, Elev: 1690ft/515m, Tel: 651-296-6157, Nearest town: Laporte. GPS: 47.118732, -94.872485

15 • B2 | Paul Bunyan SF Dispersed 3

Dispersed sites, No water, No toilets, Tent & RV camping: Free, Stay limit: 14-21 days, Reservations not accepted, Elev: 1772ft/540m, Tel: 651-296-6157, Nearest town: Akeley. GPS: 47.099353, -94.857932

16 • B2 | Paul Bunyan SF Dispersed 4

Dispersed sites, No water, No toilets, Tent & RV camping: Free, Stay limit: 14-21 days, Reservations not accepted, Elev: 1672ft/510m, Tel: 651-296-6157, Nearest town: Akeley. GPS: 47.093004, -94.787671

17 • B2 | Paul Bunyan SF Dispersed 5

Dispersed sites, No water, No toilets, Tent & RV camping: Free, Nothing larger than van/PU, Stay limit: 14-21 days, Reservations not accepted, Elev: 1490ft/454m, Tel: 651-296-6157, Nearest town: Walker. GPS: 47.102162, -94.674089

18 • B2 | Red Lake SF - Waskish

Dispersed sites, No water, Vault/pit toilet, Tent & RV camping: Free, Open May-Oct, Reservations not accepted, Elev: 1178ft/359m, Tel: 218-647-8592, Nearest town: Waseca. GPS: 48.164737, -94.508666

19 • B2 | Two Inlets SF - Hungryman Lake

Total sites: 14, RV sites: 14, Central water, Vault/pit toilet, No showers, No RV dump, Tent & RV camping: $17, Reservations not accepted, Elev: 1493ft/455m, Tel: 218-699-7201, Nearest town: Park Rapids. GPS: 47.059967, -95.182752

20 • B3 | Cloquet Vallet SF - Indian Lake CG

Total sites: 25, RV sites: 25, Central water, Vault/pit toilet, No showers, No RV dump, Tent & RV camping: $17, Max Length: 20ft, Reservations not accepted, Elev: 1515ft/462m, Tel: 218-226-6377, Nearest town: Two Harbors. GPS: 47.271699, -91.847873

21 • B3 | Cloquet Valley SF

Dispersed sites, No water, Vault/pit toilet, Tent & RV camping: Free, Elev: 1439ft/439m, Tel: 218-878-5640, Nearest town: Cotton. GPS: 47.067302, -92.232702

22 • B3 | Cloquet Valley SF - Bear Lake

Dispersed sites, No water, Vault/pit toilet, Tent & RV camping: Free, Reservations not accepted, Elev: 1502ft/458m, Tel: 218-878-5640, Nearest town: Rollins. GPS: 47.206438, -91.921768

23 • B3 | Cloquet Valley SF - Cloquet River Water Camp

Dispersed sites, No water, Vault/pit toilet, Tent & RV camping: Free, Elev: 1427ft/435m, Tel: 218-878-5640, Nearest town: Cotton. GPS: 47.115768, -92.025063

24 • B3 | Finland SF - Sullivan Lake

Total sites: 12, RV sites: 12, Central water, Vault/pit toilet, No showers, No RV dump, Tent & RV camping: $17, Reservations not accepted, Elev: 1726ft/526m, Tel: 218-226-6377, Nearest town: Two Harbors. GPS: 47.381369, -91.669063

25 • B3 | Gen. G C Andrews SF - Button Box

Total sites: 13, RV sites: 11, Central water, Vault/pit toilet, No showers, No RV dump, Tent & RV camping: $17, Reservations not accepted, Elev: 1430ft/436m, Tel: 218-254-7979, Nearest town: Togo. GPS: 47.853091, -93.286773

26 • B3 | Geo. Washington SF - Larson Lake

Total sites: 12, RV sites: 12, Central water, Vault/pit toilet, No showers, No RV dump, Tent & RV camping: $17, Max Length: 20ft, Reservations not accepted, Elev: 1417ft/432m, Tel: 218-743-3362, Nearest town: Bigfork. GPS: 47.773595, -93.416104

27 • B3 | Geo. Washington SF - Lost Lake

Total sites: 15, RV sites: 15, Central water, Vault/pit toilet, No showers, No RV dump, Tent & RV camping: $17, Max Length: 20ft, Reservations not accepted, Elev: 1391ft/424m, Tel: 218-743-3362, Nearest town: Bigfork. GPS: 47.685448, -93.405955

28 • B3 | Geo. Washington SF - Owen Lake

Total sites: 20, RV sites: 18, Central water, Vault/pit toilet, No showers, No RV dump, Tent & RV camping: $17, Also walk-to sites, Max Length: 20ft, Reservations not accepted, Elev: 1414ft/431m, Tel: 218-743-3362, Nearest town: Bigfork. GPS: 47.677580, -93.392090

29 • B3 | Geo. Washington SF - Stony Brook Horse Camp

Total sites: 17, RV sites: 17, Central water, Vault/pit toilet, No showers, No RV dump, Tent & RV camping: $22, Max Length: 20ft, Reservations not accepted, Elev: 1411ft/430m, Tel: 218-254-7979, Nearest town: Bigfork. GPS: 47.721974, -93.089133

30 • B3 | Geo. Washington SF - Thistledew Lake CG

Total sites: 21, RV sites: 21, Central water, Vault/pit toilet, No showers, No RV dump, Tent & RV camping: $17, Max Length: 20ft, Reservations not accepted, Elev: 1421ft/433m, Tel: 218-254-7979, Nearest town: Togo. GPS: 47.797591, -93.232695

31 • B3 | Geo. Washington SF - Togo Horse

Total sites: 12, RV sites: 12, Central water, Vault/pit toilet, No showers, No RV dump, Tent & RV camping: $22, Max Length: 20ft, Reservations not accepted, Elev: 1404ft/428m, Tel: 218-254-7979, Nearest town: Bigfork. GPS: 47.804607, -93.224644

32 • B3 | Kabetogama SF - Wakemup Bay CG

Total sites: 22, RV sites: 22, Central water, Vault/pit toilet, No showers, No RV dump, Tent & RV camping: $17, Reservations not accepted, Elev: 1362ft/415m, Tel: 218-365-7229, Nearest town: Cook. GPS: 47.902215, -92.603136

33 • B3 | Savanna SF - Hay Lake

Total sites: 20, RV sites: 20, Central water, Vault/pit toilet, No showers, No RV dump, Tent & RV camping: $14-15, Reservations not accepted, Elev: 1276ft/389m, Tel: 218-426-3271, Nearest town: Jacobson. GPS: 46.952536, -93.206989

34 • B4 | Finland SF - Eckbeck CG

Total sites: 31, RV sites: 31, Central water, Vault/pit toilet, No showers, No RV dump, Tent & RV camping: $17, Max Length: 21ft, Reservations not accepted, Elev: 1070ft/326m, Tel: 218-226-6365, Nearest town: Finland. GPS: 47.373251, -91.227421

35 • B4 | Finland SF - Finland CG

Total sites: 39, RV sites: 39, Central water, Vault/pit toilet, No showers, No RV dump, Tent & RV camping: $17, Max Length: 21ft, Reservations not accepted, Elev: 1319ft/402m, Tel: 218-226-6365, Nearest town: Finland. GPS: 47.413587, -91.241392

36 • B4 | Grand Portage SF - Devilfish Lake

Total sites: 5, RV sites: 5, No water, Vault/pit toilet, Tent & RV camping: Free, Reservations not accepted, Elev: 1880ft/573m, Tel: 218-387-3039, Nearest town: Grand Marais. GPS: 47.990731, -90.095206

37 • B4 | Grand Portage SF - Esther Lake

Total sites: 3, RV sites: 3, No water, Vault/pit toilet, Tent & RV camping: Free, Reservations not accepted, Elev: 1975ft/602m, Tel: 218-387-3039, Nearest town: Grand Marais. GPS: 47.981739, -90.108114

38 • B4 | Grand Portage SF - McFarland Lake

Total sites: 5, RV sites: 5, No water, Vault/pit toilet, Tent & RV camping: Free, Reservations not accepted, Elev: 1529ft/466m, Tel: 218-387-3039, Nearest town: Hovland. GPS: 48.045519, -90.057883

39 • B4 | Pat Bayle SF - Twin Lakes

Total sites: 3, RV sites: 3, No water, No toilets, Tent & RV camping: $14-15, Reservations not accepted, Elev: 1745ft/532m, Tel: 218-387-3039, Nearest town: Grand Marais. GPS: 47.983172, -90.375504

40 • C2 | Birch Lakes SF

Total sites: 29, RV sites: 29, Central water, Vault/pit toilet, No showers, No RV dump, Tent & RV camping: $17, Open May-Oct, Reservations not accepted, Elev: 1204ft/367m, Tel: 320-616-2525, Nearest town: Melrose. GPS: 45.772421, -94.771660

41 • C2 | Crow Wing SF - Greer Lake CG

Total sites: 31, RV sites: 31, Central water, Vault/pit toilet, No showers, No RV dump, Tent & RV camping: $17, Max Length: 20ft, Reservations not accepted, Elev: 1220ft/372m, Tel: 218-546-5926, Nearest town: Crosby. GPS: 46.632972, -94.040033

42 • C2 | Foothills SF

Dispersed sites, No water, Tent & RV camping: Free, Reservations not accepted, Elev: 1425ft/434m, Tel: 218-947-3232, Nearest town: Pine River. GPS: 46.721759, -94.618370

43 • C2 | Huntersville SF - Landing (77.7R)

Total sites: 24, RV sites: 24, Central water, Vault/pit toilet, No showers, No RV dump, Tent & RV camping: $17, Also boat-in sites, Elev: 1355ft/413m, Tel: 218-266-2100, Nearest town: Huntersville. GPS: 46.738328, -94.928802

44 • C2 | Huntersville SF - Shell City Horse Camp

Total sites: 35, RV sites: 8, Central water, Vault/pit toilet, No showers, No RV dump, Tent & RV camping: $17, 27 horse sites, Reservations not accepted, Elev: 1368ft/417m, Tel: 218-266-2100, Nearest town: Menagha. GPS: 46.791619, -94.947305

45 • C2 | Huntersville SF - Shell City Landing

Total sites: 19, RV sites: 19, Central water, Vault/pit toilet, No showers, No RV dump, Tent & RV camping: $17, Elev: 1384ft/422m, Tel: 218-266-2100, Nearest town: Sebeka. GPS: 46.792237, -94.949853

46 • C2 | Land O'Lakes SF Dispersed 1

Dispersed sites, No water, No toilets, Tent & RV camping: Free, Reservations not accepted, Elev: 1477ft/450m, Tel: 651-296-6157, Nearest town: Pine River. GPS: 46.813121, -94.171216

47 • C2 | Pillsbury SF - Rock Lake CG

Total sites: 48, RV sites: 48, Central water, Vault/pit toilet, No showers, No RV dump, Tent & RV camping: $17, Max Length: 20ft, Reservations not accepted, Elev: 1293ft/394m, Tel: 218-825-3075, Nearest town: Pillager. GPS: 46.429436, -94.481151

48 • C2 | Pillsbury SF - Walter E Stark Horse Camp

Total sites: 25, RV sites: 25, Central water, Vault/pit toilet, No showers, No RV dump, Tent & RV camping: $22, Reservations not accepted, Elev: 1375ft/419m, Tel: 218-825-3075, Nearest town: Pillager. GPS: 46.376885, -94.452358

49 • C2 | Rum River SF - Esker Trail Dispersed

Dispersed sites, No water, No toilets, Tent & RV camping: Free, Stay limit: 14-21 days, Reservations not accepted, Elev: 1195ft/364m, Tel: 320-616-2450, Nearest town: Ogilvie. GPS: 45.885859, -93.559513

50 • C2 | Rum River SF - Game Refuge Rd

Dispersed sites, No water, No toilets, Tent & RV camping: Free, Nothing larger than van/PU, Stay limit: 14-21 days, Reservations not accepted, Elev: 1238ft/377m, Tel: 320-616-2450, Nearest town: Ogilvie. GPS: 45.925273, -93.574177

51 • C2 | Rum River SF - Kanabec Forest Rd Dispersed 1

Dispersed sites, No water, No toilets, Tent & RV camping: Free, Nothing larger than van/PU, Stay limit: 14-21 days, Reservations not accepted, Elev: 1191ft/363m, Tel: 320-616-2450, Nearest town: Ogilvie. GPS: 45.918234, -93.514681

52 • C2 | Rum River SF - Kanabec Forest Rd Dispersed 2

Dispersed sites, No water, No toilets, Tent & RV camping: Free, Stay limit: 14-21 days, Reservations not accepted, Elev: 1144ft/349m, Tel: 320-616-2450, Nearest town: Ogilvie. GPS: 45.883898, -93.505152

53 • C2 | Rum River SF - Riders Trail Dispersed

Dispersed sites, No water, No toilets, Tent & RV camping: Free, Stay limit: 14-21 days, Reservations not accepted, Elev: 1220ft/372m, Tel: 320-616-2450, Nearest town: Ogilvie. GPS: 45.934926, -93.559199

54 • C2 | Rum River SF - Unnamed Rd Dispersed 1

Dispersed sites, No water, No toilets, Tent & RV camping: Free, Nothing larger than van/PU, Stay limit: 14-21 days, Reservations not accepted, Elev: 1131ft/345m, Tel: 320-616-2450, Nearest town: Ogilvie. GPS: 45.854003, -93.554066

55 • C2 | Sand Dunes SF - Ann Lake

Total sites: 30, RV sites: 30, Central water, Vault/pit toilet, No showers, No RV dump, Tent & RV camping: $17, Max Length: 20ft, Reservations not accepted, Elev: 974ft/297m, Tel: 763-878-2325, Nearest town: Zimmerman. GPS: 45.426758, -93.693359

56 • C2 | Sand Dunes SF - Bob Dunn Horse Camp

Total sites: 15, RV sites: 15, Central water, Vault/pit toilet, No showers, No RV dump, Tent & RV camping: $22, Reservations not accepted, Elev: 971ft/296m, Tel: 763-878-2325, Nearest town: Zimmerman. GPS: 45.433927, -93.708731

57 • C3 | Chengwatana SF - Snake River CG

Total sites: 28, RV sites: 26, Central water, Vault/pit toilet, No showers, No RV dump, Tent & RV camping: $14, Max Length: 20ft, Elev: 843ft/257m, Tel: 651-583-2125, Nearest town: Pine City. GPS: 45.822110, -92.780240

58 • C3 | Gen. G C Andrews SF - Willow River

Total sites: 38, RV sites: 38, Central water, Vault/pit toilet, No showers, No RV dump, Tent & RV camping: $17, Max Length: 22ft, Reservations not accepted, Elev: 1066ft/325m, Tel: 218-485-5400, Nearest town: Willow River. GPS: 46.327187, -92.826611

59 • C3 | Nemadji SF - Garfvert CG

Total sites: 19, RV sites: 18, Central water, Vault/pit toilet, No showers, No RV dump, Tent & RV camping: $14-15, Also boat-in sites, Reservations not accepted, Elev: 1171ft/357m, Tel: 218-485-5420, Nearest town: Nickerson. GPS: 46.405285, -92.440083

60 • C3 | St Croix SF - Boulder

Total sites: 22, RV sites: 22, Central water, Vault/pit toilet, No showers, No RV dump, Tent & RV camping: $14-15, Reservations not accepted, Elev: 994ft/303m, Tel: 320-384-6146, Nearest town: Hinckley. GPS: 46.049161, -92.418174

61 • C3 | St Croix SF - Tamarack Horse Camp

Total sites: 56, RV sites: 56, Central water, Vault/pit toilet, No showers, No RV dump, Tent & RV camping: $24, 2 family sites @ $12 each, Reservations not accepted, Elev: 928ft/283m, Tel: 320-384-6591, Nearest town: Hinckley. GPS: 46.064358, -92.386677

62 • D3 | Richard J. Dorer SF - Kruger CG

Total sites: 19, RV sites: 19, Central water, Vault/pit toilet, No showers, No RV dump, Tent & RV camping: $17, Generator hours: 0800-2200, Reservations not accepted, Elev: 778ft/237m, Tel: 651-345-3401, Nearest town: Wabasha. GPS: 44.339482, -92.075771

63 • D3 | Richard J. Dorer SF - Zumbro Bottom Horse Camp Central

Total sites: 16, RV sites: 16, Central water, Vault/pit toilet, No showers, No RV dump, Tent & RV camping: $22, Open all year, Reservations not accepted, Elev: 718ft/219m, Tel: 651-345-3401, Nearest town: Reno. GPS: 44.301275, -92.122584

64 • D3 | Richard J. Dorer SF - Zumbro Bottom Horse Camp North

Total sites: 6, RV sites: 6, Central water, Vault/pit toilet, No showers, No RV dump, Tent & RV camping: $22, Open all year, Reservations not accepted, Elev: 732ft/223m, Tel: 651-345-3401, Nearest town: Reno. GPS: 44.322317, -92.129888

65 • D3 | Richard J. Dorer SF - Zumbro Bottom Horse Camp West

Total sites: 50, RV sites: 50, Central water, Vault/pit toilet, No showers, No RV dump, Tent & RV camping: $22, Open all year, Reservations not accepted, Elev: 758ft/231m, Tel: 651-345-3401, Nearest town: Reno. GPS: 44.316456, -92.145694

66 • E3 | Richard J. Dorer SF - Money Creek/Vinegar Ridge

Total sites: 8, RV sites: 8, No water, Vault/pit toilet, Tent & RV camping: $17, Reservations not accepted, Elev: 850ft/259m, Tel: 507-724-2107, Nearest town: Houston. GPS: 43.783344, -91.674714

67 • E3 | Richard J. Dorer SF - Oak Ridge/Wet Bark

Total sites: 5, RV sites: 5, No water, Vault/pit toilet, Tent & RV camping: $17, Open all year, Reservations not accepted, Elev: 1168ft/356m, Tel: 507-724-2107, Nearest town: Houston. GPS: 43.737938, -91.642602

68 • E4 | Richard J. Dorer SF - Reno Horse Camp

Total sites: 11, RV sites: 5, No water, Vault/pit toilet, Tent & RV camping: $22, 6 horse sites, Open all year, Reservations not accepted, Elev: 715ft/218m, Tel: 507-724-2107, Nearest town: Reno. GPS: 43.605349, -91.280851

Missouri

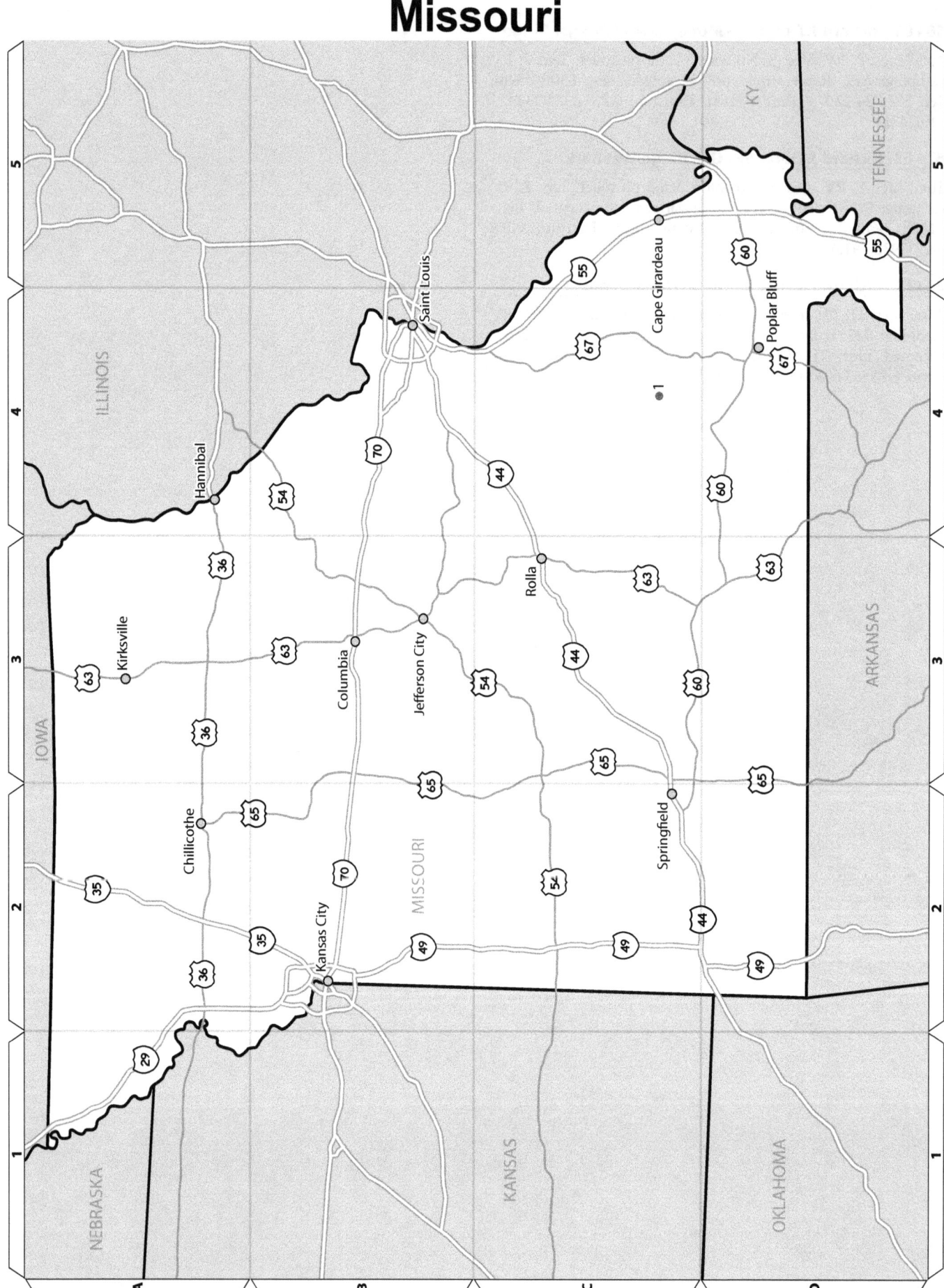

Map	ID	Map	ID
C4	1		

Alphabetical List of Camping Areas

Name   **ID**   **Map**

Funk Memorial SF - MDC .... 1 .... C4

1 • C4 | Funk Memorial SF - MDC

Dispersed sites, No water, No toilets, Tent & RV camping: Free, Reservations not accepted, Elev: 1106ft/337m, Tel: 573-223-4525, Nearest town: Vulcan. GPS: 37.312074, -90.722218

Montana

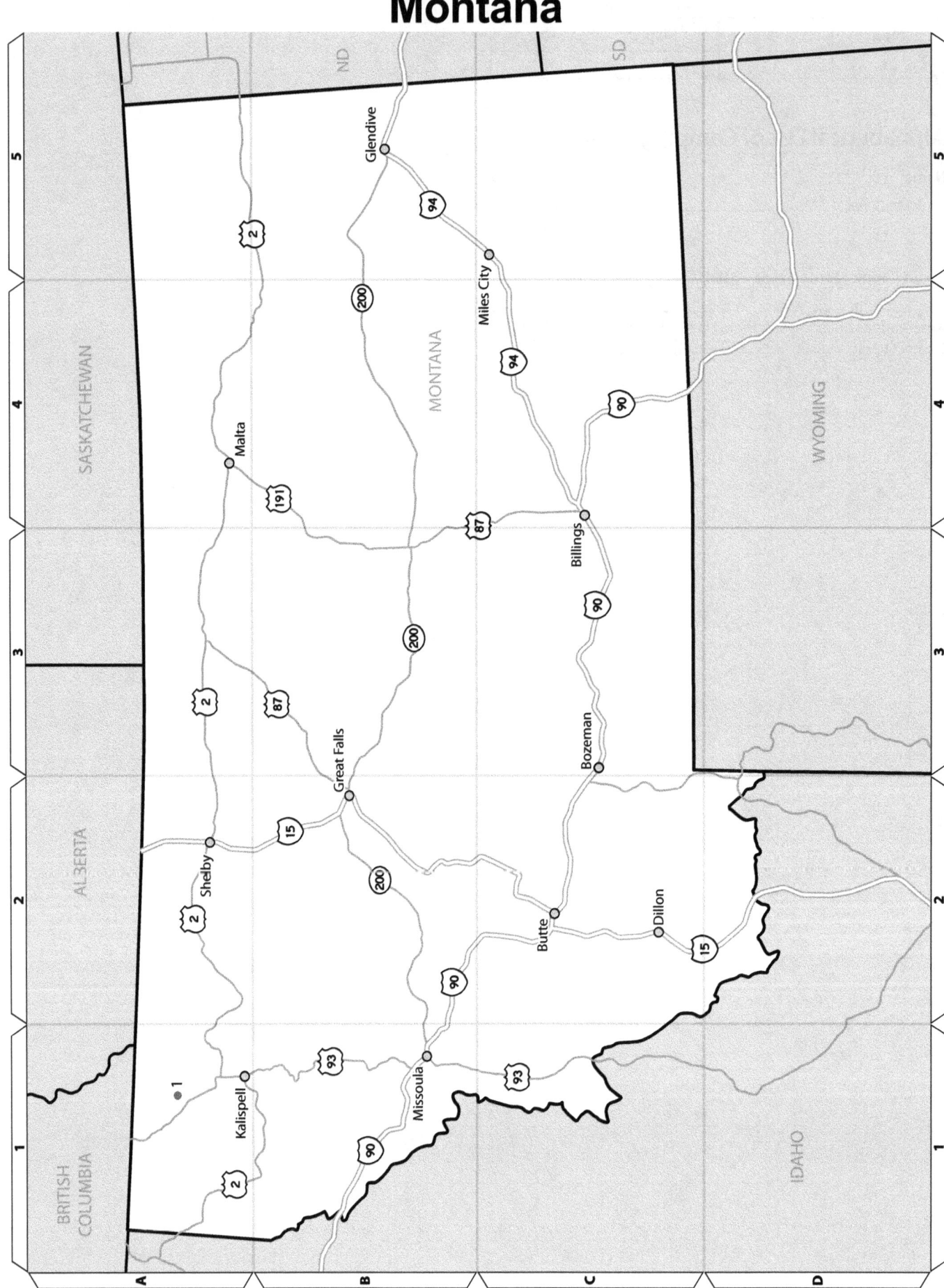

Map	ID	Map	ID
A1	1		

Alphabetical List of Camping Areas

Name   **ID**   **Map**

Upper Whitefish Lake - DNRC .... 1 .... A1

1 • A1 | Upper Whitefish Lake - DNRC

Total sites: 15, RV sites: 10, No water, Vault/pit toilet, No showers, No RV dump, Tent & RV camping: Free, Stay limit: 14 days, Generator hours: 0800-2200, Open Jun-Oct, Reservations not accepted, Elev: 4472ft/1363m, Tel: 406-881-2371, Nearest town: Olney. GPS: 48.684779, -114.574654

New Hampshire

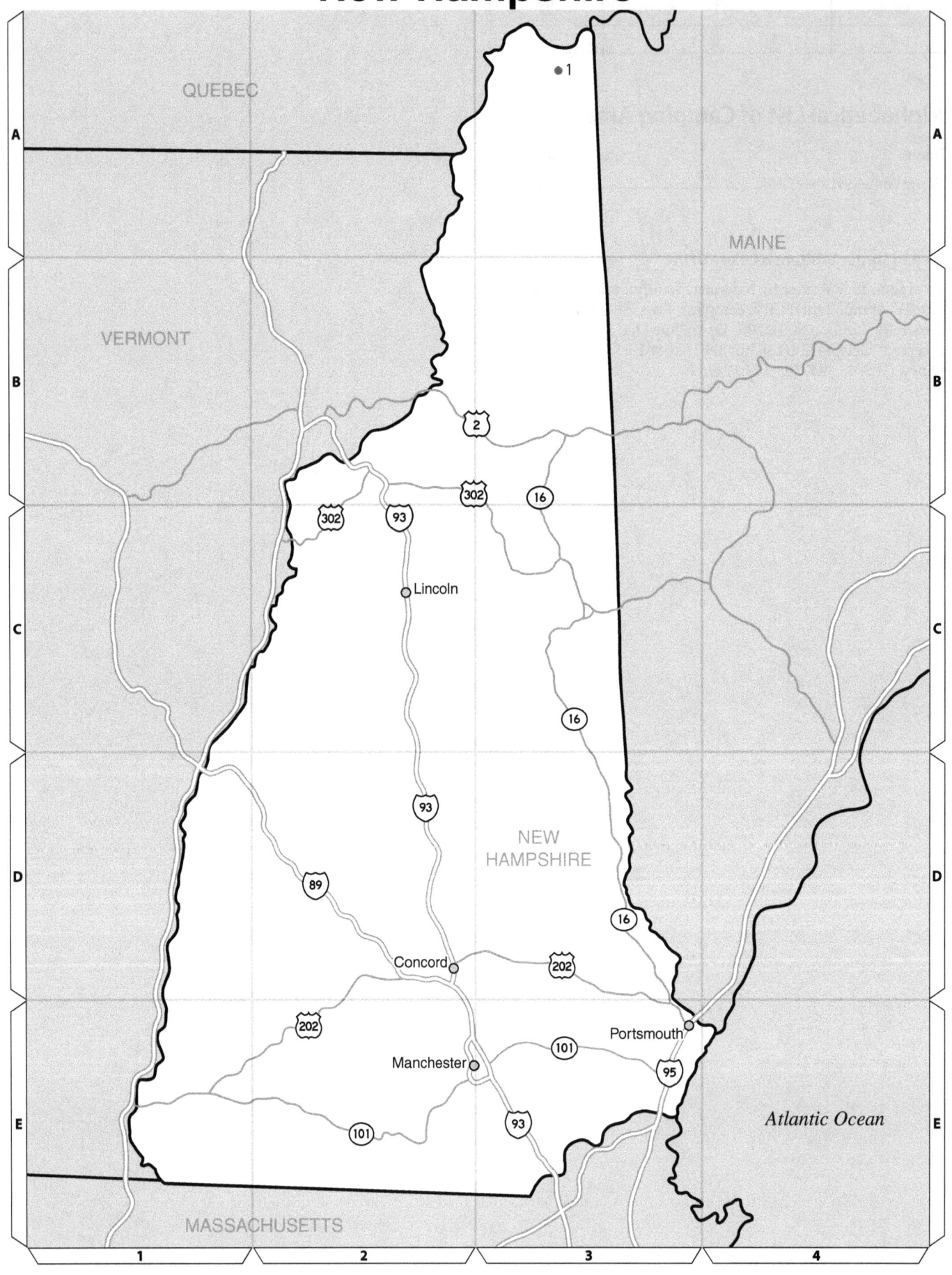

Map	ID	Map	ID
A3	1		

Alphabetical List of Camping Areas

Name .... **ID** .... **Map**

Deer Mountain - Ct Lakes SF .... 1 .... A3

1 • A3 | Deer Mountain - Ct Lakes SF

Total sites: 25, RV sites: 14, Central water, Vault/pit toilet, No showers, No RV dump, Tent & RV camping: $23, Tent/popups only, Open May-Oct, Elev: 1968ft/600m, Tel: 603-538-6965, Nearest town: Pittsburg. GPS: 45.190674, -71.190674

New Jersey

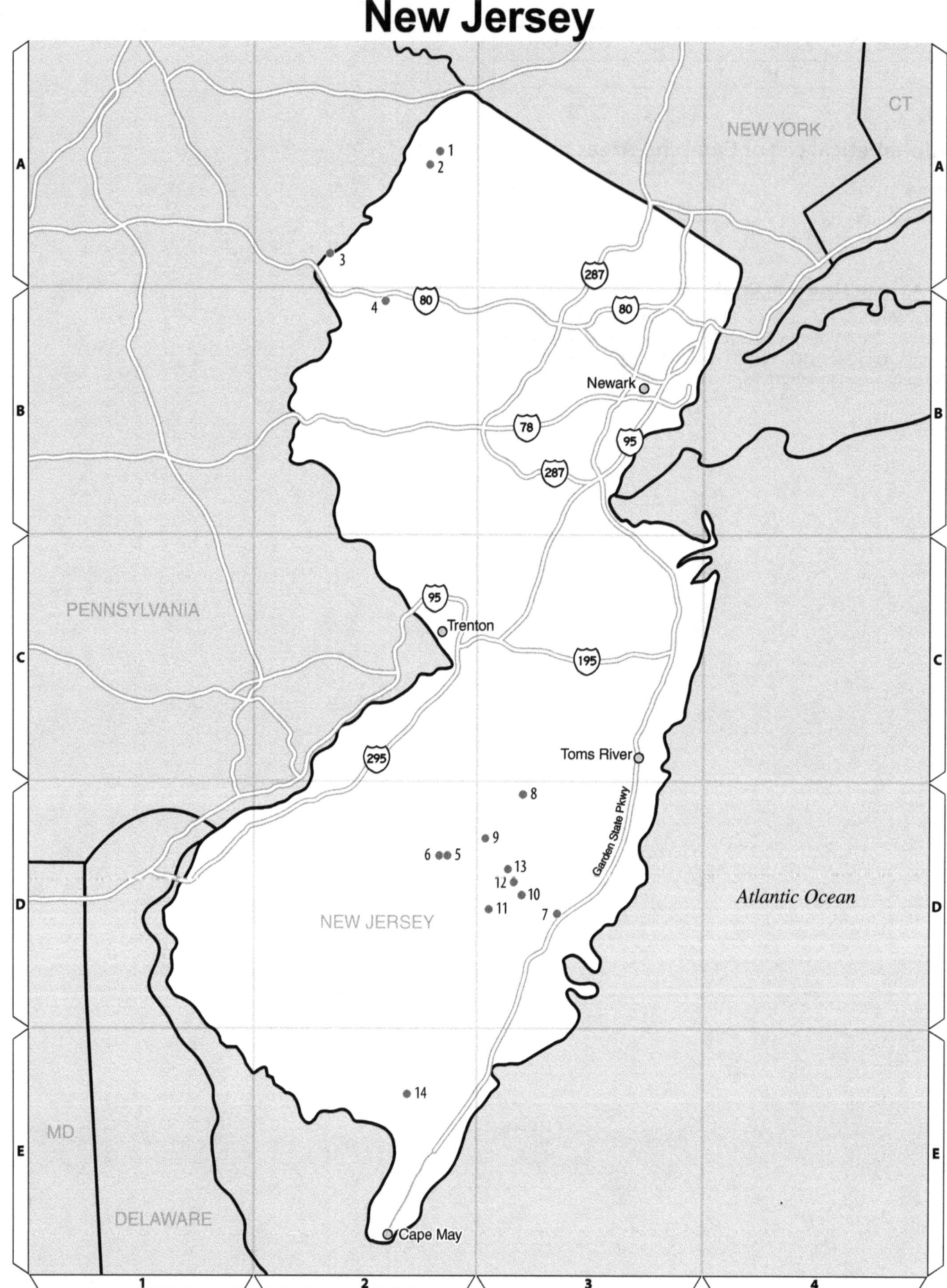

Map	ID	Map	ID
A2	1-3	D3	7-13
B2	4	E2	14
D2	5-6		

Alphabetical List of Camping Areas

Name	ID	Map
Bass River SF	7	D3
Belleplain SF	14	E2
Brendan T. Byrne SF	8	D3
Jenny Jump SF	4	B2
Stokes SF - Lake Ocquittunk	1	A2
Stokes SF - Shotwell	2	A2
Wharton SF - Atsion	5	D2
Wharton SF - Batona	9	D3
Wharton SF - Bodine Field	10	D3
Wharton SF - Buttonwood Hill	11	D3
Wharton SF - Godfrey Bridge	12	D3
Wharton SF - Goshen Pond	6	D2
Wharton SF - Hawkins Bridge	13	D3
Worthington SF	3	A2

1 • A2 | Stokes SF - Lake Ocquittunk

Total sites: 24, RV sites: 24, Central water, No toilets, No showers, No RV dump, Tent & RV camping: $25, Also cabins, NJ residents: $20, Open all year, Reservations accepted, Elev: 774ft/236m, Tel: 973-948-3820, Nearest town: Branchville. GPS: 41.227732, -74.762344

2 • A2 | Stokes SF - Shotwell

Total sites: 27, RV sites: 27, Central water, No toilets, No showers, No RV dump, Tent & RV camping: $25, NJ residents: $20, Open all year, Reservations accepted, Elev: 837ft/255m, Tel: 973-948-3820, Nearest town: Branchville. GPS: 41.200071, -74.794635

3 • A2 | Worthington SF

Total sites: 69, RV sites: 46, Central water, Flush toilet, Free showers, No RV dump, Tent & RV camping: $25, NJ residents: $20, 3 group sites: $70-$140, Open Apr-Dec, Reservations accepted, Elev: 338ft/103m, Tel: 908-841-9575, Nearest town: Columbia. GPS: 41.012734, -75.086102

4 • B2 | Jenny Jump SF

Total sites: 22, RV sites: 19, Central water, Flush toilet, Free showers, Tent & RV camping: $25, NJ residents: $20, 2 group sites: $50-$160, Open Apr-Oct, Reservations accepted, Elev: 876ft/267m, Tel: 908-459-4366, Nearest town: Hope. GPS: 40.913939, -74.921191

5 • D2 | Wharton SF - Atsion

Total sites: 50, RV sites: 50, Central water, Flush toilet, Free showers, RV dump, Tent & RV camping: $25, NJ residents: $20, Open Apr-Oct, Reservations accepted, Elev: 76ft/23m, Tel: 609-268-0444, Nearest town: Atsion. GPS: 39.744722, -74.742449

6 • D2 | Wharton SF - Goshen Pond

Dispersed sites, Central water, Vault/pit toilet, Tent & RV camping: $3-5, Elev: 89ft/27m, Tel: 609-268-0444, Nearest town: Atsion. GPS: 39.745391, -74.760389

7 • D3 | Bass River SF

Total sites: 176, RV sites: 176, Central water, Flush toilet, Free showers, RV dump, Tent & RV camping: $25, Also group sites & cabins, NJ residents: $20, Group sites: $50-$100, Open all year, Reservations accepted, Elev: 30ft/9m, Tel: 609-296-1114, Nearest town: Tuckerton. GPS: 39.621375, -74.423185

8 • D3 | Brendan T. Byrne SF

Total sites: 79, RV sites: 79, Flush toilet, Free showers, Tent & RV camping: $25, NJ residents: $20, 3 group sites: $60-$120, Open all year, Reservations accepted, Elev: 144ft/44m, Tel: 609-726-1191, Nearest town: Woodland Township. GPS: 39.871879, -74.521924

9 • D3 | Wharton SF - Batona

Dispersed sites, Central water, Vault/pit toilet, Tent & RV camping: $3-5, Elev: 76ft/23m, Tel: 609-268-0444, Nearest town: Atsion. GPS: 39.780861, -74.631879

10 • D3 | Wharton SF - Bodine Field

Dispersed sites, Central water, Vault/pit toilet, Tent & RV camping: $3-5, Elev: 26ft/8m, Tel: 609-268-0444, Nearest town: Atsion. GPS: 39.660474, -74.525414

11 • D3 | Wharton SF - Buttonwood Hill

Dispersed sites, No water, Vault/pit toilet, Tent & RV camping: $3-5, Max Length: 20ft, Elev: 56ft/17m, Tel: 609-268-0444, Nearest town: Atsion. GPS: 39.628953, -74.617873

12 • D3 | Wharton SF - Godfrey Bridge

Total sites: 34, RV sites: 34, Central water, Vault/pit toilet, No showers, No RV dump, Tent & RV camping: $3-5, Group sites: $30-$200, Open all year, Max Length: 21ft, Reservations accepted, Elev: 56ft/17m, Tel: 609-268-0444, Nearest town: Atsion. GPS: 39.689243, -74.549324

13 • D3 | Wharton SF - Hawkins Bridge

Dispersed sites, Central water, Vault/pit toilet, Tent & RV camping: $3-5, Elev: 52ft/16m, Tel: 609-268-0444, Nearest town: Atsion. GPS: 39.714428, -74.565872

14 • E2 | Belleplain SF

Total sites: 169, RV sites: 169, Central water, Flush toilet, Free showers, RV dump, Tent & RV camping: $25, NJ residents: $20, 2 group sites: $100-$200, Open all year, Reservations accepted, Elev: 52ft/16m, Tel: 609-861-2404, Nearest town: Woodbine. GPS: 39.244597, -74.854844

New York

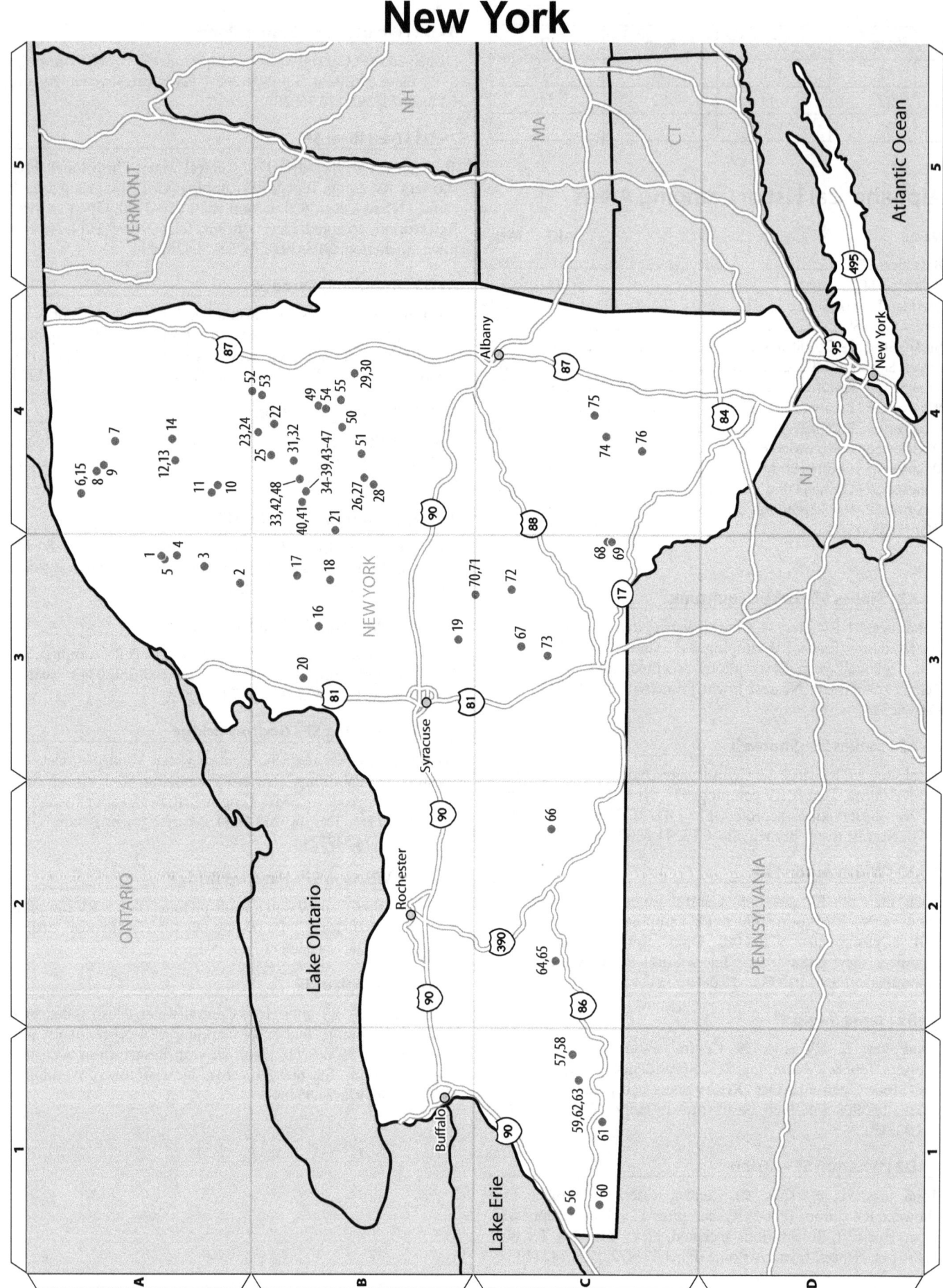

Map	ID	Map	ID
A3	1-5	C1	56-63
A4	6-15	C2	64-66
B3	16-20	C3	67-73
B4	21-55	C4	74-76

Alphabetical List of Camping Areas

Name	ID	Map
Allaben - DEC	74	C4
Balsam Swamp SF - Balsam Pond	67	C3
Bear Spring Mountain - Launt Pond - NY DEC	68	C3
Bear Spring Mountain - Spruce Grove - NY DEC	69	C3
Black River Wild Forest - North Lake Dispersed	21	B4
Blue Mountain Wild Forest - Chain Lake Road Dispersed 2	22	B4
Blue Mountain Wild Forest - Cornell Road Dispersed 3	23	B4
Blue Mountain Wild Forest - Cornell Road Dispersed 4	24	B4
Blue Ridge Wilderness - Durant Road Dispersed	25	B4
Brasher SF - Walter Pratt Memorial Park	6	A4
Charles Baker SF - Moscow Hill Assembly Area	70	C3
Charles Baker SF - Moscow Hill Horse Camp	71	C3
Chautauqua Gorge SF	56	C1
Deer River SF	7	A4
Deer River SF - Horse Assembly Area	8	A4
Deer River SF - Iron Bridge	9	A4
Devils Tombstone - DEC	75	C4
Downerville SF - River PFAR	1	A3
Ferris Lake Wild Forest - Powley Rd Dispersed 1	26	B4
Ferris Lake Wild Forest - Powley Rd Dispersed 2	27	B4
Ferris Lake Wild Forest - Powley Rd Dispersed 3	28	B4
Fish Creek SF - East Branch Dispersed	16	B3
Frank E Jadwin Memorial State Forest - Blanchard Creek Rd	2	A3
Golden Hill SF - Chapman Road	57	C1
Golden Hill SF - Firelane Road	58	C1
Greenwood State Forest - Site 4	3	A3
Horseshoe Lake Wild Forest - Horseshoe Lake 7	10	A4
Horseshoe Lake Wild Forest - Otterbrook Road 11	11	A4
Hunts Pond SF	72	C3
Independence River Wild Forest - Partridgeville Road Dispersed	17	B3
Jersey Hill SF - Fire Tower	64	C2
Jersey Hill SF - Scholes Rd 2	65	C2
Lake George Wild Forest - Bear Slide Road Dispersed 17	29	B4
Lake George Wild Forest - Buttermilk Road Dispersed 6	30	B4
Long Pond SF	73	C3
McCarty Hill SF - Mutton Hollow Road	59	C1
Moose River Plains - Cedar River Flow - DEC	31	B4
Moose River Plains - Wakely Pond - DEC	32	B4
Moose River Plains Wild Forest - Limekiln Lake Rd Dispersed 23	33	B4
Moose River Plains Wild Forest - Limekiln Lake Rd Dispersed 48-49	34	B4
Moose River Plains Wild Forest - Limekiln Lake Rd Dispersed 52	35	B4
Moose River Plains Wild Forest - Limekiln Lake Rd Dispersed 53-55	36	B4
Moose River Plains Wild Forest - Limekiln Lake Rd Dispersed 57-58	37	B4
Moose River Plains Wild Forest - Limekiln Lake Rd Dispersed 59-61	38	B4
Moose River Plains Wild Forest - Limekiln Lake Rd Dispersed 64	39	B4
Moose River Plains Wild Forest - Limekiln Lake Rd Dispersed 76	40	B4
Moose River Plains Wild Forest - Limekiln Lake Rd Dispersed 77	41	B4
Moose River Plains Wild Forest - Moose River Rd Dispersed 22	42	B4
Moose River Plains Wild Forest - Moose River Rd Dispersed 66 (Otter Brook)	43	B4
Moose River Plains Wild Forest - Otter Brook Rd Dispersed 101	44	B4
Moose River Plains Wild Forest - Otter Brook Rd Dispersed 89	45	B4
Moose River Plains Wild Forest - Otter Brook Rd Dispersed 89	46	B4
Moose River Plains Wild Forest - Otter Brook Rd Dispersed 98	47	B4
Moose River Plains Wild Forest - Limekiln Lake Rd Dispersed 7	48	B4
North Harmony SF - Wiltsie Road	60	C1
Peekamoose Valley - DEC	76	C4
Pine Hill SF - Pineapple Junction	61	C1
Rock City SF - Camp Seneca	62	C1
Rock City SF - Hale Road	63	C1
Sand Flats SF - Corners Rd Dispersed	18	B3
Saranac Lakes Wild Forest - Floodwood Road 17	12	A4
Saranac Lakes Wild Forest - Floodwood Road 18	13	A4
Saranac Lakes Wild Forest - Little Green Pond 4-6	14	A4
Siamese Ponds Wilderness - 11th Mt TH	49	B4
Siamese Ponds Wilderness - Augur Falls Dispersed	50	B4
Silver Hill SF - McCarthy Road	4	A3
Silver Lake Wilderness - Whitehouse Dispersed 2-3	51	B4
Stoney Pond SF	19	B3
Sugar Hill SF - Fire Tower	66	C2
Vanderwhacker Mountain Wild Forest - Blue Ridge Road Dispersed 1	52	B4
Vanderwhacker Mountain Wild Forest - Boreas River Dispersed 1-2	53	B4
Walter Pratt Memorial Park - DEC	15	A4
Whippoorwill Corners SF - Burnell Access	5	A3
Wilcox Lake Wild Forest - Rt 8 Campsite 003	54	B4
Wilcox Lake Wild Forest - West Stony Creek Rd Dispersed 2	55	B4
Winona SF - Bargy Road Middle	20	B3

1 • A3 | Downerville SF - River PFAR

Dispersed sites, No water, Tent & RV camping: Free, Open all year, Reservations not accepted, Elev: 684ft/208m, Tel: 315-265-3090, Nearest town: Russell. GPS: 44.425775, -75.107431

2 • A3 | Frank E Jadwin Memorial State Forest - Blanchard Creek Road

Dispersed sites, No water, No toilets, Tent & RV camping: Free, Open all year, Reservations not accepted, Elev: 928ft/283m, Tel: 315-376-3521, Nearest town: Harrisville. GPS: 44.016991, -75.321405

3 • A3 | Greenwood State Forest - Site 4

Dispersed sites, No water, No toilets, Tent & RV camping: Free, Only small RVs, Open all year, Reservations not accepted, Elev: 1040ft/317m, Tel: 607-622-8282, Nearest town: Harrisville. GPS: 44.204027, -75.197667

4 • A3 | Silver Hill SF - McCarthy Road

Dispersed sites, No water, No toilets, Tent & RV camping: Free, Open all year, Reservations not accepted, Elev: 789ft/240m, Tel: 315-265-3090, Nearest town: Degrasse. GPS: 44.347674, -75.110272

5 • A3 | Whippoorwill Corners SF - Burnell Access

Dispersed sites, No water, No toilets, Tent & RV camping: Free, No large RVs, Open all year, Reservations not accepted, Elev: 634ft/193m, Tel: 315-265-3090, Nearest town: Russell. GPS: 44.411114, -75.146778

6 • A4 | Brasher SF - Walter Pratt Memorial Park

Total sites: 21, RV sites: 12, No water, No toilets, Tent & RV camping: Free, 21 sites along road around pond, Open all year, Reservations not accepted, Elev: 262ft/80m, Tel: 315-265-3090, Nearest town: North Lawrence. GPS: 44.836439, -74.673879

7 • A4 | Deer River SF

Dispersed sites, No toilets, Tent & RV camping: Free, Elev: 1519ft/463m, Tel: 518-897-1200, Nearest town: Dickinson Center. GPS: 44.657125, -74.305582

8 • A4 | Deer River SF - Horse Assembly Area

Dispersed sites, No water, No toilets, Tent & RV camping: Free, Open all year, Reservations not accepted, Elev: 942ft/287m, Tel: 518-897-1200, Nearest town: Dickinson Center. GPS: 44.751521, -74.513261

9 • A4 | Deer River SF - Iron Bridge

Dispersed sites, No water, No toilets, Tent & RV camping: Free, Nothing larger than van/PU, Open all year, Reservations not accepted, Elev: 1234ft/376m, Tel: 518-897-1200, Nearest town: Dickinson Center. GPS: 44.719277, -74.480003

10 • A4 | Horseshoe Lake Wild Forest - Horseshoe Lake 7

Dispersed sites, No water, No toilets, Tent & RV camping: Free, Open all year, Reservations not accepted, Elev: 1744ft/532m, Tel: 315-265-3090, Nearest town: Tupper Lake. GPS: 44.134414, -74.629875

11 • A4 | Horseshoe Lake Wild Forest - Otterbrook Road 11

Dispersed sites, No water, No toilets, Tent & RV camping: Free, Open all year, Reservations not accepted, Elev: 1741ft/531m, Tel: 315-265-3090, Nearest town: Tupper Lake. GPS: 44.160058, -74.677361

12 • A4 | Saranac Lakes Wild Forest - Floodwood Road 17

Dispersed sites, No water, No toilets, Tent & RV camping: Free, Open all year, Reservations not accepted, Elev: 1634ft/498m, Tel: 518-897-1200, Nearest town: Lake Placid. GPS: 44.346305, -74.442995

13 • A4 | Saranac Lakes Wild Forest - Floodwood Road 18

Dispersed sites, No water, No toilets, Tent & RV camping: Free, Open all year, Reservations not accepted, Elev: 1630ft/497m, Tel: 518-897-1200, Nearest town: Lake Placid. GPS: 44.344912, -74.445015

14 • A4 | Saranac Lakes Wild Forest - Little Green Pond 4-6

Dispersed sites, No water, No toilets, Tent & RV camping: Free, 3 sites along E shore, Open all year, Reservations not accepted, Elev: 1644ft/501m, Tel: 518-897-1200, Nearest town: Lake Placid. GPS: 44.357557, -74.296145

15 • A4 | Walter Pratt Memorial Park - DEC

Dispersed sites, No toilets, Tent & RV camping: Free, Generator hours: 0900-1100/1600-1900, Elev: 295ft/90m, Tel: 315-265-3090, Nearest town: North Lawrence. GPS: 44.835736, -74.672794

16 • B3 | Fish Creek SF - East Branch Dispersed

Dispersed sites, No water, No toilets, Tent & RV camping: Free, Open all year, Reservations not accepted, Elev: 1735ft/529m, Tel: 315-866-6330, Nearest town: Constableville. GPS: 43.603989, -75.616803

17 • B3 | Independence River Wild Forest - Partridgeville Road Dispersed

Dispersed sites, No water, Tent & RV camping: Free, Max Length: 20ft, Reservations not accepted, Elev: 1285ft/392m, Tel: 315-376-3521, Nearest town: Lowville. GPS: 43.716007, -75.262465

18 • B3 | Sand Flats SF - Corners Rd Dispersed

Dispersed sites, No water, No toilets, Tent & RV camping: Free, Open all year, Reservations not accepted, Elev: 1100ft/335m, Tel: 315-376-3521, Nearest town: Boonville. GPS: 43.555012, -75.288844

19 • B3 | Stoney Pond SF

Total sites: 17, RV sites: 15, No water, Vault/pit toilet, No showers, No RV dump, Tent & RV camping: Free, Also walk-to sites, 2 walk-to sites, Permit required, Open all year, Reservations accepted, Elev: 1549ft/472m, Tel: 607-674-4017, Nearest town: Morrisville. GPS: 42.880547, -75.715882

20 • B3 | Winona SF - Bargy Road Middle

Dispersed sites, No water, Tent & RV camping: Free, Open all year, Elev: 1143ft/348m, Tel: 315-376-3521, Nearest town: Mannsville. GPS: 43.696342, -75.975833

21 • B4 | Black River Wild Forest - North Lake Dispersed

Dispersed sites, No water, No toilets, Tent & RV camping: Free, 10 sites along road, Reservations not accepted, Elev: 1830ft/558m, Tel: 315-866-6330, Nearest town: Forestport. GPS: 43.523521, -74.949426

22 • B4 | Blue Mountain Wild Forest - Chain Lake Road Dispersed 2

Dispersed sites, No water, No toilets, Tent & RV camping: Free, Open all year, Reservations not accepted, Elev: 1560ft/475m, Tel: 518-863-4545, Nearest town: Indian Lake. GPS: 43.832493, -74.207951

23 • B4 | Blue Mountain Wild Forest - Cornell Rd Dispersed 3

Dispersed sites, No water, No toilets, Tent & RV camping: Free, Nothing larger than van/PU, Open all year, Reservations not accepted, Elev: 1776ft/541m, Tel: 518-863-4545, Nearest town: Indian Lake. GPS: 43.912983, -74.262259

24 • B4 | Blue Mountain Wild Forest - Cornell Rd Dispersed 4

Dispersed sites, No water, No toilets, Tent & RV camping: Free, Open all year, Reservations not accepted, Elev: 1631ft/497m, Tel: 518-863-4545, Nearest town: Indian Lake. GPS: 43.913244, -74.255606

25 • B4 | Blue Ridge Wilderness - Durant Road Dispersed

Dispersed sites, No water, No toilets, Tent & RV camping: Free, Open all year, Reservations not accepted, Elev: 1775ft/541m, Tel: 518-863-4545, Nearest town: Blue Mountain Lake. GPS: 43.847123, -74.422556

26 • B4 | Ferris Lake Wild Forest - Powley Rd Dispersed 1

Dispersed sites, No water, No toilets, Tent & RV camping: Free, Many other sites along 10 miles of road, Open all year, Reservations not accepted, Elev: 1807ft/551m, Tel: 518-863-4545, Nearest town: Higgins Bay. GPS: 43.360949, -74.589359

27 • B4 | Ferris Lake Wild Forest - Powley Rd Dispersed 2

Dispersed sites, No water, No toilets, Tent & RV camping: Free, Many other sites along 10 miles of road, Open all year, Reservations not accepted, Elev: 1838ft/560m, Tel: 518-863-4545, Nearest town: Higgins Bay. GPS: 43.349623, -74.614252

28 • B4 | Ferris Lake Wild Forest - Powley Rd Dispersed 3

Dispersed sites, No water, No toilets, Tent & RV camping: Free, Many other sites along 10 miles of road, Open all year, Reservations not accepted, Elev: 1671ft/509m, Tel: 518-863-4545, Nearest town: Higgins Bay. GPS: 43.313308, -74.651532

29 • B4 | Lake George Wild Forest - Bear Slide Rd Dispersed 17

Dispersed sites, No water, No toilets, Tent & RV camping: Free, Permit required, Open all year, Elev: 735ft/224m, Nearest town: Lake Luzerne. GPS: 43.397519, -73.874892

30 • B4 | Lake George Wild Forest - Buttermilk Rd Dispersed 6

Dispersed sites, No water, No toilets, Tent & RV camping: Free, Open all year, Reservations not accepted, Elev: 630ft/192m, Tel: 518-623-1200, Nearest town: Lake Luzerne. GPS: 43.400923, -73.880134

31 • B4 | Moose River Plains - Cedar River Flow - DEC

Total sites: 8, RV sites: 7, No water, No toilets, Tent & RV camping: Free, Winter access by foot or snowmobile, Open all year, Elev: 2116ft/645m, Tel: 518-863-4545, Nearest town: Indian Lake. GPS: 43.726296, -74.473356

32 • B4 | Moose River Plains - Wakely Pond- DEC

Dispersed sites, No toilets, Tent & RV camping: Free, Winter access by foot or snowmobile, Open all year, Elev: 2129ft/649m, Tel: 518-863-4545, Nearest town: Indian Lake. GPS: 43.737941, -74.464119

33 • B4 | Moose River Plains Wild Forest - Limekiln Lake Rd Dispersed 23

Dispersed sites, No water, No toilets, Tent & RV camping: Free, Winter access by foot or snowmobile, Open all year, Reservations not accepted, Elev: 2055ft/626m, Tel: 518-863-4545, Nearest town: Inlet. GPS: 43.693328, -74.604084

34 • B4 | Moose River Plains Wild Forest - Limekiln Lake Rd Dispersed 48-49

Dispersed sites, No water, No toilets, Tent & RV camping: Free, Winter access by foot or snowmobile, Open all year, Reservations not accepted, Elev: 1878ft/572m, Tel: 518-863-4545, Nearest town: Inlet. GPS: 43.681946, -74.666679

35 • B4 | Moose River Plains Wild Forest - Limekiln Lake Rd Dispersed 52

Dispersed sites, No water, No toilets, Tent & RV camping: Free, Winter access by foot or snowmobile, Open all year, Reservations not accepted, Elev: 1860ft/567m, Tel: 518-863-4545, Nearest town: Inlet. GPS: 43.675161, -74.681913

36 • B4 | Moose River Plains Wild Forest - Limekiln Lake Rd Dispersed 53-55

Dispersed sites, No water, No toilets, Tent & RV camping: Free, No large RVs, Open all year, Reservations not accepted, Elev: 1873ft/571m, Tel: 518-863-4545, Nearest town: Inlet. GPS: 43.673489, -74.682223

37 • B4 | Moose River Plains Wild Forest - Limekiln Lake Rd Dispersed 57-58

Dispersed sites, No water, No toilets, Tent & RV camping: Free, Winter access by foot or snowmobile, Open all year, Reservations not accepted, Elev: 1861ft/567m, Tel: 518-863-4545, Nearest town: Inlet. GPS: 43.673539, -74.690725

38 • B4 | Moose River Plains Wild Forest - Limekiln Lake Rd Dispersed 59-61

Dispersed sites, No water, No toilets, Tent & RV camping: Free, Winter access by foot or snowmobile, Open all year, Reservations not accepted, Elev: 1870ft/570m, Tel: 518-863-4545, Nearest town: Inlet. GPS: 43.672659, -74.691569

39 • B4 | Moose River Plains Wild Forest - Limekiln Lake Rd Dispersed 64

Dispersed sites, No water, No toilets, Tent & RV camping: Free, Winter access by foot or snowmobile, Open all year, Reservations not accepted, Elev: 1851ft/564m, Tel: 518-863-4545, Nearest town: Inlet. GPS: 43.674376, -74.709091

40 • B4 | Moose River Plains Wild Forest - Limekiln Lake Rd Dispersed 76

Dispersed sites, No water, No toilets, Tent & RV camping: Free, Winter access by foot or snowmobile, Open all year, Reservations not accepted, Elev: 1886ft/575m, Tel: 518-863-4545, Nearest town: Inlet. GPS: 43.686252, -74.747237

41 • B4 | Moose River Plains Wild Forest - Limekiln Lake Rd Dispersed 77

Dispersed sites, No water, No toilets, Tent & RV camping: Free,

Winter access by foot or snowmobile, Open all year, Reservations not accepted, Elev: 1888ft/575m, Tel: 518-863-4545, Nearest town: Inlet. GPS: 43.689256, -74.749896

42 • B4 | Moose River Plains Wild Forest - Moose River Rd Dispersed 22

Dispersed sites, No water, No toilets, Tent & RV camping: Free, Winter access by foot or snowmobile, Open all year, Reservations not accepted, Elev: 2048ft/624m, Tel: 518-863-4545, Nearest town: Indian Lake. GPS: 43.693804, -74.603199

43 • B4 | Moose River Plains Wild Forest - Moose River Rd Dispersed 66 (Otter Brook)

Dispersed sites, No water, No toilets, Tent & RV camping: Free, Nothing larger than van/PU, Winter access by foot or snowmobile, Open all year, Reservations not accepted, Elev: 1862ft/568m, Tel: 518-863-4545, Nearest town: Inlet. GPS: 43.676549, -74.708071

44 • B4 | Moose River Plains Wild Forest - Otter Brook Rd Dispersed 101

Dispersed sites, No toilets, Tent & RV camping: Free, Numerous nearby sites, Winter access by foot or snowmobile, Open all year, Elev: 1899ft/579m, Nearest town: Inlet. GPS: 43.656393, -74.693835

45 • B4 | Moose River Plains Wild Forest - Otter Brook Rd Dispersed 89

Dispersed sites, No toilets, Tent & RV camping: Free, Winter access by foot or snowmobile, Open all year, Elev: 1853ft/565m, Nearest town: Inlet. GPS: 43.659743, -74.700398

46 • B4 | Moose River Plains Wild Forest - Otter Brook Rd Dispersed 89

Dispersed sites, No water, No toilets, Tent & RV camping: Free, Winter access by foot or snowmobile, Open all year, Reservations not accepted, Elev: 1872ft/571m, Tel: 518-863-4545, Nearest town: Inlet. GPS: 43.658272, -74.700898

47 • B4 | Moose River Plains Wild Forest - Otter Brook Rd Dispersed 98

Dispersed sites, No water, No toilets, Tent & RV camping: Free, Winter access by foot or snowmobile, Open all year, Reservations not accepted, Elev: 1870ft/570m, Tel: 518-863-4545, Nearest town: Inlet. GPS: 43.658792, -74.696627

48 • B4 | Moose River Plains Wild Forest - Limekiln Lake Rd Dispersed 7

Dispersed sites, No water, No toilets, Tent & RV camping: Free, No large RVs, Winter access by foot or snowmobile, Open all year, Reservations not accepted, Elev: 2246ft/685m, Tel: 518-863-4545, Nearest town: Inlet. GPS: 43.703846, -74.580949

49 • B4 | Siamese Ponds Wilderness - 11th Mt TH

Dispersed sites, No water, No toilets, Tent & RV camping: Free, Open all year, Reservations not accepted, Elev: 1777ft/542m, Tel: 518-623-1200, Nearest town: Speculator. GPS: 43.590392, -74.090306

50 • B4 | Siamese Ponds Wilderness - Augur Falls Dispersed

Dispersed sites, No water, No toilets, Tent & RV camping: Free, Open all year, Reservations not accepted, Elev: 1368ft/417m, Tel: 518-623-1200, Nearest town: Northville. GPS: 43.471172, -74.251676

51 • B4 | Silver Lake Wilderness - Whitehouse Dispersed 2-3

Dispersed sites, No water, No toilets, Tent & RV camping: Free, Open all year, Reservations not accepted, Elev: 1290ft/393m, Tel: 518-863-4545, Nearest town: Speculator. GPS: 43.371169, -74.429086

52 • B4 | Vanderwhacker Mountain Wild Forest - Blue Ridge Road Dispersed 1

Dispersed sites, No water, No toilets, Tent & RV camping: Free, Nothing larger than van/PU, Open all year, Reservations not accepted, Elev: 1938ft/591m, Tel: 518-623-1200, Nearest town: Newcomb. GPS: 43.942594, -73.977955

53 • B4 | Vanderwhacker Mountain Wild Forest - Boreas River Dispersed 1-2

Dispersed sites, No water, No toilets, Tent & RV camping: Free, 2 separated sites, Open all year, Reservations not accepted, Elev: 1624ft/495m, Tel: 518-623-1200, Nearest town: Newcomb. GPS: 43.891939, -74.014103

54 • B4 | Wilcox Lake Wild Forest - Rt 8 Campsite 003

Dispersed sites, No water, No toilets, Tent & RV camping: Free, Open all year, Reservations not accepted, Elev: 1405ft/428m, Tel: 518-897-1200, Nearest town: Speculator. GPS: 43.561766, -74.116889

55 • B4 | Wilcox Lake Wild Forest - West Stony Creek Rd Dispersed 2

Dispersed sites, No water, No toilets, Tent & RV camping: Free, Open all year, Reservations not accepted, Elev: 1515ft/462m, Tel: 518-897-1200, Nearest town: Warrensburg. GPS: 43.480511, -74.062663

56 • C1 | Chautauqua Gorge SF

Total sites: 8, RV sites: 1, No water, Tent & RV camping: Free, Open all year, Max Length: 18ft, Reservations not accepted, Elev: 1449ft/442m, Tel: 716-363-2052, Nearest town: Mayville. GPS: 42.240105, -79.585066

57 • C1 | Golden Hill SF - Chapman Road

Dispersed sites, No water, No toilets, Tent & RV camping: Free, Open all year, Reservations not accepted, Elev: 2157ft/657m, Tel: 716-372-0645, Nearest town: Rushford. GPS: 42.252905, -78.524025

58 • C1 | Golden Hill SF - Firelane Road

Dispersed sites, No water, No toilets, Tent & RV camping: Free, Open all year, Reservations not accepted, Elev: 2251ft/686m, Tel: 716-372-0645, Nearest town: Rushford. GPS: 42.257325, -78.524674

59 • C1 | McCarty Hill SF - Mutton Hollow Road

Dispersed sites, No water, No toilets, Tent & RV camping: Free,

Open all year, Reservations not accepted, Elev: 1844ft/562m, Tel: 716-372-0645, Nearest town: Ellicottville. GPS: 42.241646, -78.686089

60 • C1 | North Harmony SF - Wiltsie Road

Dispersed sites, No water, No toilets, Tent & RV camping: Free, Several sites along road, Open all year, Reservations not accepted, Elev: 1735ft/529m, Tel: 716-363-2052, Nearest town: Panama. GPS: 42.088452, -79.529343

61 • C1 | Pine Hill SF - Pineapple Junction

Dispersed sites, No water, No toilets, Tent & RV camping: Free, Open all year, Reservations not accepted, Elev: 2094ft/638m, Tel: 716-363-2052, Nearest town: Randolph. GPS: 42.090749, -78.978096

62 • C1 | Rock City SF - Camp Seneca

Dispersed sites, No water, No toilets, Tent & RV camping: Free, Open all year, Reservations not accepted, Elev: 1742ft/531m, Tel: 716-372-0645, Nearest town: Ellicottville. GPS: 42.224417, -78.700108

63 • C1 | Rock City SF - Hale Road

Dispersed sites, No water, No toilets, Tent & RV camping: Free, Open all year, Reservations not accepted, Elev: 1712ft/522m, Tel: 716-372-0645, Nearest town: Ellicottville. GPS: 42.210666, -78.700931

64 • C2 | Jersey Hill SF - Fire Tower

Dispersed sites, No water, No toilets, Tent & RV camping: Free, Open all year, Elev: 2246ft/685m, Tel: 585-466-3241, Nearest town: Almond. GPS: 42.351956, -77.884547

65 • C2 | Jersey Hill SF - Scholes Rd 2

Dispersed sites, No water, No toilets, Tent & RV camping: Free, Open all year, Reservations not accepted, Elev: 1817ft/554m, Tel: 585-466-3241, Nearest town: Almond. GPS: 42.354289, -77.905207

66 • C2 | Sugar Hill SF - Fire Tower

Dispersed sites, Central water, Flush toilet, Tent & RV camping: Free, Horse stalls, Reservations not accepted, Elev: 2087ft/636m, Tel: 607-776-2165, Nearest town: Watkins Glen. GPS: 42.386734, -77.002486

67 • C3 | Balsam Swamp SF - Balsam Pond

Dispersed sites, No water, Vault/pit toilet, Tent & RV camping: Free, Open all year, Elev: 1707ft/520m, Tel: 607-674-4017, Nearest town: Norwich. GPS: 42.549092, -75.758251

68 • C3 | Bear Spring Mountain - Launt Pond - NY DEC

Total sites: 27, RV sites: 27, Central water, Flush toilet, Free showers, RV dump, Tent & RV camping: $23, Open May-Sep, Reservations accepted, Elev: 2205ft/672m, Tel: 607-865-6989, Nearest town: Downsville. GPS: 42.103516, -75.069336

69 • C3 | Bear Spring Mountain - Spruce Grove - NY DEC

Total sites: 14, RV sites: 14, Central water, No toilets, No showers, No RV dump, Tent & RV camping: $23, Horse camp, Open May-Sep, Reservations accepted, Elev: 1339ft/408m, Tel: 607-865-6989, Nearest town: Downsville. GPS: 42.074207, -75.058399

70 • C3 | Charles Baker SF - Moscow Hill Assembly Area

Dispersed sites, No water, Vault/pit toilet, Tent & RV camping: Free, Open May-Oct, Reservations not accepted, Elev: 1436ft/438m, Nearest town: Sangerfield. GPS: 42.791359, -75.407363

71 • C3 | Charles Baker SF - Moscow Hill Horse Camp

Dispersed sites, No water, Vault/pit toilet, Tent & RV camping: Free, Open all year, Reservations not accepted, Elev: 1451ft/442m, Nearest town: Sangerfield. GPS: 42.793506, -75.406138

72 • C3 | Hunts Pond SF

Total sites: 18, No water, Tent & RV camping: Free, Permit required May-Sep, Stay limit: 14 days, Open May-Sep, Reservations accepted, Elev: 1522ft/464m, Tel: 518-408-5850, Nearest town: New Berlin. GPS: 42.594727, -75.372559

73 • C3 | Long Pond SF

Total sites: 10, RV sites: 10, No water, Vault/pit toilet, Tent & RV camping: Free, Open all year, Elev: 1252ft/382m, Tel: 607-674-4017, Nearest town: Smithville Flats. GPS: 42.417102, -75.834847

74 • C4 | Allaben - DEC

Dispersed sites, No water, No toilets, Tent & RV camping: Free, Generator hours: 0900-1100/1600-1900, Elev: 1109ft/338m, Tel: 845-256-3000, Nearest town: Phoenicia. GPS: 42.109507, -74.350568

75 • C4 | Devils Tombstone - DEC

Total sites: 24, RV sites: 24, No toilets, Tent & RV camping: $21, NY residents: $5 discount, Generator hours: 0900-1100/1600-1900, Open May-Sep, Reservations accepted, Elev: 2044ft/623m, Tel: 845-688-7160, Nearest town: Hunter. GPS: 42.159679, -74.203484

76 • C4 | Peekamoose Valley - DEC

Dispersed sites, No toilets, Tent & RV camping: Free, Generator hours: 0900-1100/1600-1900, Elev: 1204ft/367m, Tel: 845-256-3000, Nearest town: West Shokan. GPS: 41.915999, -74.443352

North Dakota

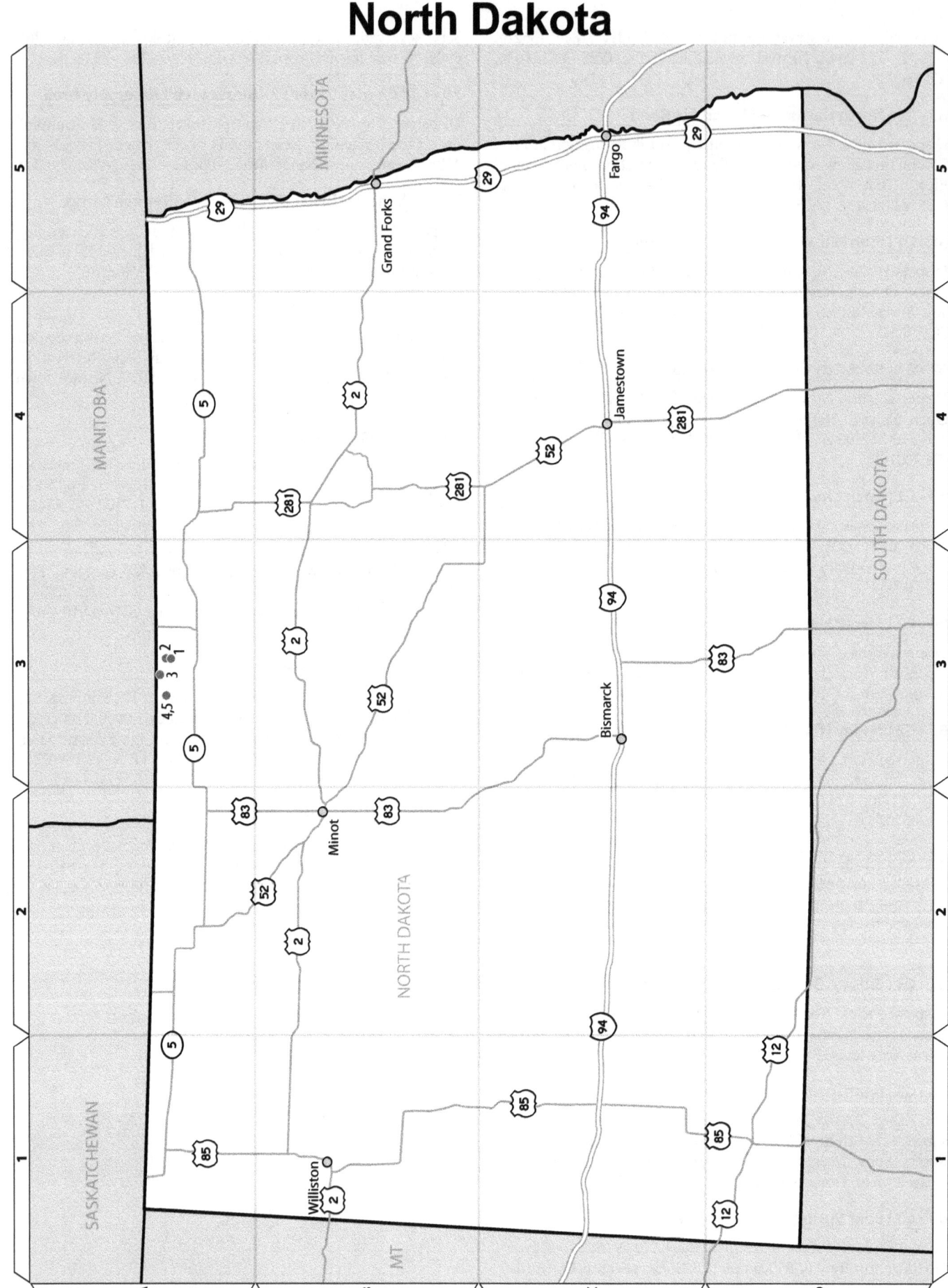

Map	ID	Map	ID
A3	1-5		

Alphabetical List of Camping Areas

Name	ID	Map
Homen SF - Long Lake Access	1	A3
Homen SF - Pelican Lake	2	A3
Turtle Mountain SF - Hahn's Bay	3	A3
Turtle Mountain SF - Strawberry Lake RA	4	A3
Turtle Mountain SF - Twisted Oaks Horse Camp	5	A3

1 • A3 | Homen SF - Long Lake Access

Dispersed sites, Central water, Vault/pit toilet, Tent & RV camping: Free, Elev: 2175ft/663m, Tel: 701-228-3700, Nearest town: Bottineau. GPS: 48.928733, -100.264221

2 • A3 | Homen SF - Pelican Lake

Dispersed sites, Central water, Vault/pit toilet, Tent & RV camping: $15, Elev: 2221ft/677m, Tel: 701-228-3700, Nearest town: Bottineau. GPS: 48.946317, -100.265268

3 • A3 | Turtle Mountain SF - Hahn's Bay

Total sites: 8, RV sites: 8, No water, No toilets, Tent & RV camping: $15, Stay limit: 14 days, Generator hours: 0600-2300, Elev: 2156ft/657m, Tel: 701-228-3700, Nearest town: Bottineau. GPS: 48.970855, -100.364891

4 • A3 | Turtle Mountain SF - Strawberry Lake RA

Total sites: 9, RV sites: 9, No water, No toilets, Tent & RV camping: $15, Stay limit: 14 days, Generator hours: 0600-2300, Elev: 2201ft/671m, Tel: 701-228-3700, Nearest town: Bottineau. GPS: 48.946333, -100.508554

5 • A3 | Turtle Mountain SF - Twisted Oaks Horse Camp

Total sites: 5, RV sites: 5, Central water, No toilets, No showers, No RV dump, Tent & RV camping: $15, Plus $5/horse, Stay limit: 14 days, Generator hours: 0600-2300, Elev: 2113ft/644m, Tel: 701-228-3700, Nearest town: Bottineau. GPS: 48.946985, -100.523183

Ohio

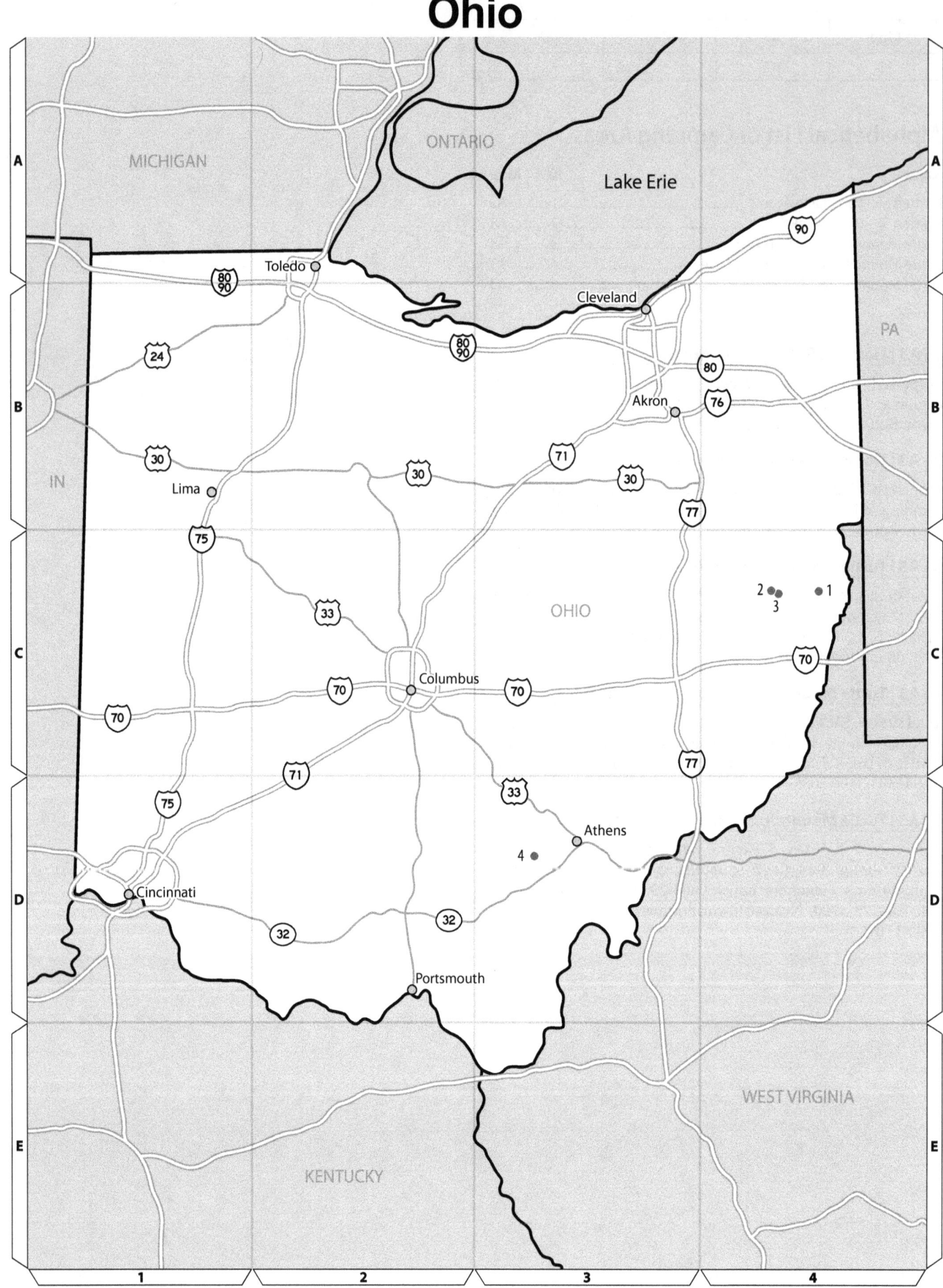

Van and RV Camping in State Forests

Map	ID	Map	ID
C4	1-4		

Alphabetical List of Camping Areas

Name	ID	Map
Fernwood SF - Hidden Hollow CG	1	C4
Harrison County SF - Ronsheim CG	2	C4
Harrison County SF - Trailriders CG	3	C4
Zaleski SF - Horse Camp	4	D3

1 • C4 | Fernwood SF - Hidden Hollow CG

Total sites: 22, RV sites: 22, Central water, Vault/pit toilet, No showers, No RV dump, Tent & RV camping: Free, Elev: 1174ft/358m, Tel: 740-266-6021, Nearest town: Bloomingdale. GPS: 40.334439, -80.764145

2 • C4 | Harrison County SF - Ronsheim CG

Total sites: 7, RV sites: 7, Central water, Vault/pit toilet, No showers, No RV dump, Tent & RV camping: Free, Elev: 1122ft/342m, Tel: 740-266-6021, Nearest town: Cadiz. GPS: 40.329255, -80.987879

3 • C4 | Harrison County SF - Trailriders CG

Total sites: 20, RV sites: 20, Central water, Vault/pit toilet, No showers, No RV dump, Tent & RV camping: Free, Elev: 1040ft/317m, Tel: 740-266-6021, Nearest town: Cadiz. GPS: 40.338904, -81.024907

4 • D3 | Zaleski SF - Horse Camp

Total sites: 16, RV sites: 16, No water, Vault/pit toilet, Tent & RV camping: Free, Stock water, Open all year, Elev: 1017ft/310m, Tel: 740-596-5781, Nearest town: Zaleski. GPS: 39.275406, -82.321385

Oregon

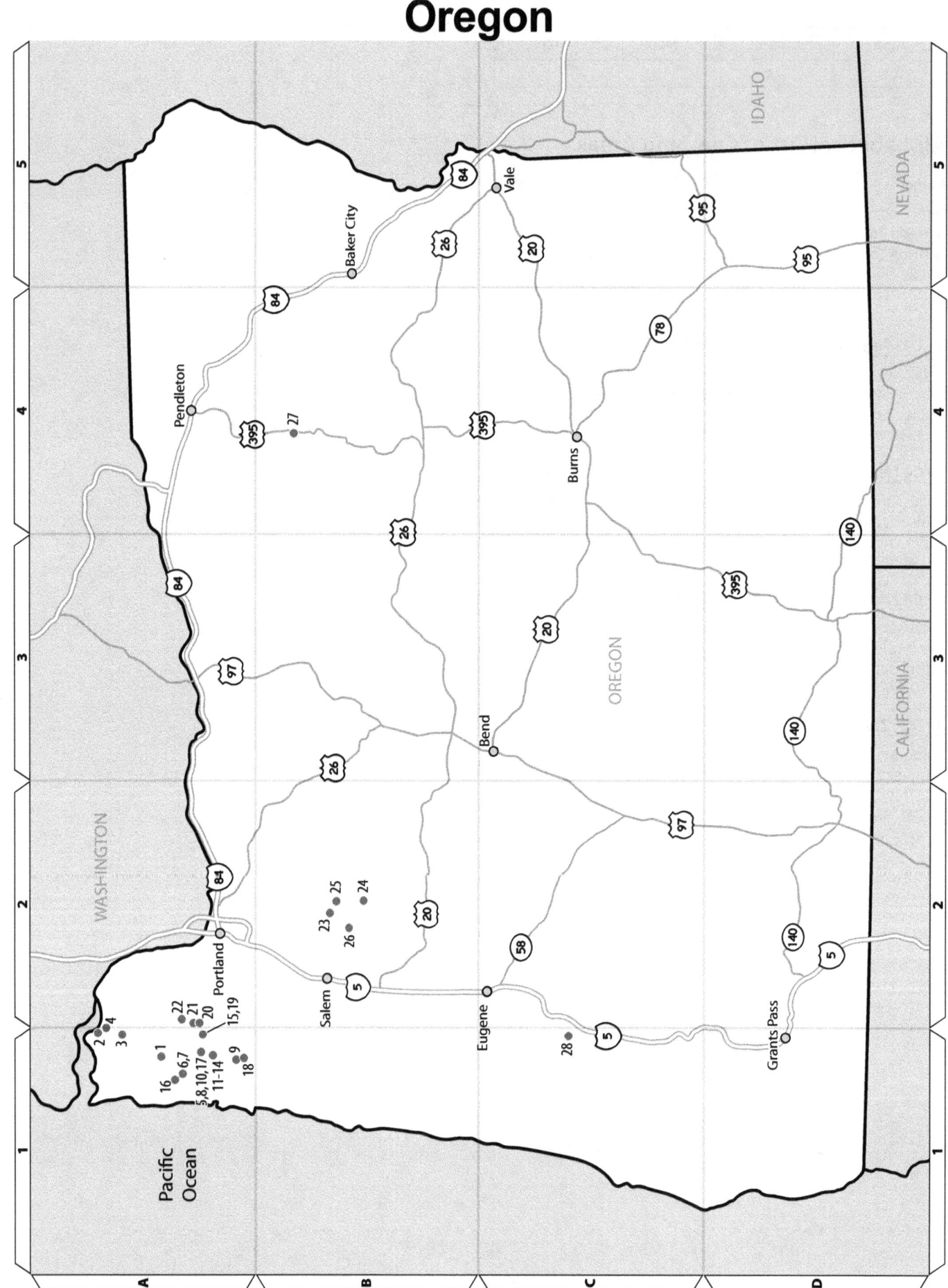

Map	ID	Map	ID
A1	1-19	B4	27
A2	20-22	C1	28
B2	23-26		

Alphabetical List of Camping Areas

Name	ID	Map
Brown's OHV Camp - SF	28	C1
Clatsop SF - Henry Rierson Spruce Run	1	A1
Clatsop SF - Kerry Road	2	A1
Clatsop SF - Northrup Creek Horse Camp	3	A1
Clatsop SF - Viewpoint	4	A1
Santiam SF - Butte Creek Falls	23	B2
Santiam SF - Horse Camp	24	B2
Santiam SF - Rhody Lake	25	B2
Santiam SF - Shellburg Falls	26	B2
Tillamook SF - Browns OHV Camp	20	A2
Tillamook SF - Cedar Creek OHV Staging Area	5	A1
Tillamook SF - Cook Creek 1	6	A1
Tillamook SF - Cook Creek 2	7	A1
Tillamook SF - Diamond Mill	8	A1
Tillamook SF - Gales Creek	21	A2
Tillamook SF - Hollywood/Edwards Creek	9	A1
Tillamook SF - Jones Creek	10	A1
Tillamook SF - Jordan Creek 1-2	11	A1
Tillamook SF - Jordan Creek 3	12	A1
Tillamook SF - Jordan Creek 6-7	13	A1
Tillamook SF - Jordan Creek OHV	14	A1
Tillamook SF - Lyda Camp	15	A1
Tillamook SF - Nehalem Falls	16	A1
Tillamook SF - North Fork Wilson	17	A1
Tillamook SF - Reehers Horse Camp	22	A2
Tillamook SF - South Fork Trask	18	A1
Tillamook SF - Stagecoach Horse Camp	19	A1
Ukiah-Dale Forest State Scenic Corridor	27	B4

1 • A1 | Clatsop SF - Henry Rierson Spruce Run

Total sites: 37, RV sites: 32, No water, Vault/pit toilet, No showers, No RV dump, Tents: $15/RVs: $20, No services in winter, Open all year, Reservations not accepted, Elev: 538ft/164m, Tel: 503-325-5451, Nearest town: Lukarilla. GPS: 45.812136, -123.611941

2 • A1 | Clatsop SF - Kerry Road

Total sites: 2, RV sites: 2, No water, Tent & RV camping: Free, Reservations not accepted, Elev: 1099ft/335m, Tel: 503-325-5451, Nearest town: Westport. GPS: 46.145415, -123.449054

3 • A1 | Clatsop SF - Northrup Creek Horse Camp

Total sites: 11, RV sites: 8, Central water, Vault/pit toilet, No showers, No RV dump, Tent & RV camping: $20, 5 equestrian sites, Open May-Nov, Reservations not accepted, Elev: 666ft/203m, Tel: 503-325-5451, Nearest town: Birkenfeld. GPS: 46.023233, -123.455996

4 • A1 | Clatsop SF - Viewpoint

Total sites: 4, RV sites: 4, No water, Vault/pit toilet, Tent & RV camping: $20, Open Apr-Oct, Reservations not accepted, Elev: 2272ft/693m, Tel: 503-325-5451, Nearest town: Clatskanie. GPS: 46.114225, -123.425859

5 • A1 | Tillamook SF - Cedar Creek OHV Staging Area

Total sites: 24, RV sites: 24, No water, Vault/pit toilet, Tent & RV camping: $5, Open all year, Reservations not accepted, Elev: 627ft/191m, Tel: 503-842-2545, Nearest town: Tillamook. GPS: 45.587033, -123.585864

6 • A1 | Tillamook SF - Cook Creek 1

Dispersed sites, No water, Tent & RV camping: Free, Elev: 96ft/29m, Tel: 503-842-2545, Nearest town: Mohler. GPS: 45.699573, -123.744807

7 • A1 | Tillamook SF - Cook Creek 2

Dispersed sites, No water, Tent & RV camping: Free, Elev: 128ft/39m, Tel: 503-842-2545, Nearest town: Mohler. GPS: 45.696924, -123.737649

8 • A1 | Tillamook SF - Diamond Mill

Total sites: 17, RV sites: 17, No water, Vault/pit toilet, Tent & RV camping: $5, Open all year, Max Length: 40ft, Reservations not accepted, Elev: 755ft/230m, Tel: 503-842-2545, Nearest town: Tillamook. GPS: 45.603983, -123.547745

9 • A1 | Tillamook SF - Hollywood/Edwards Creek

Total sites: 3, RV sites: 3, No water, No toilets, Tent & RV camping: Free, Reservations not accepted, Elev: 435ft/133m, Tel: 503-842-2545, Nearest town: Tillamook. GPS: 45.410176, -123.611879

10 • A1 | Tillamook SF - Jones Creek

Total sites: 42, RV sites: 28, Central water, Vault/pit toilet, No showers, No RV dump, Tents: $15/RVs: $20, Also walk-to & group sites, 1 group site - fee: $50, 14, Open May-Sep, Reservations not accepted, Elev: 620ft/189m, Tel: 503-842-2545, Nearest town: Tillamook. GPS: 45.589121, -123.558155

11 • A1 | Tillamook SF - Jordan Creek 1-2

Dispersed sites, No water, No toilets, Tent & RV camping: Free, Elev: 442ft/135m, Tel: 503-842-2545, Nearest town: Tillamook. GPS: 45.538731, -123.589473

12 • A1 | Tillamook SF - Jordan Creek 3

Dispersed sites, No water, No toilets, Tent & RV camping: Free, Elev: 410ft/125m, Tel: 503-842-2545, Nearest town: Tillamook. GPS: 45.544811, -123.597048

13 • A1 | Tillamook SF - Jordan Creek 6-7

Dispersed sites, No water, No toilets, Tent & RV camping: Free, Elev: 607ft/185m, Tel: 503-842-2545, Nearest town: Tillamook. GPS: 45.533293, -123.547985

14 • A1 | Tillamook SF - Jordan Creek OHV

Total sites: 6, RV sites: 6, No water, Vault/pit toilet, Tent & RV camping: $20, Open May-Sep, Max Length: 40ft, Reservations not accepted, Elev: 620ft/189m, Tel: 503-842-2545, Nearest town: Tillamook. GPS: 45.537092, -123.566986

15 • A1 | Tillamook SF - Lyda Camp

Dispersed sites, No water, Vault/pit toilet, Tent & RV camping: Free, Elev: 1142ft/348m, Tel: 503-842-2545, Nearest town: Forest Grove. GPS: 45.587816, -123.441013

16 • A1 | Tillamook SF - Nehalem Falls

Total sites: 20, RV sites: 14, Central water, Vault/pit toilet, No showers, No RV dump, Tents: $15/RVs: $20, Also walk-to sites, 6 walk-to sites, Group site available, Open May-Sep, Reservations not accepted, Elev: 177ft/54m, Tel: 503-842-2545, Nearest town: Nehalem. GPS: 45.729173, -123.771497

17 • A1 | Tillamook SF - North Fork Wilson

Dispersed sites, No water, No toilets, Tent & RV camping: $5, 7 sites, Open all year, Max Length: 18ft, Reservations not accepted, Elev: 719ft/219m, Tel: 503-842-2545, Nearest town: Tillamook. GPS: 45.611643, -123.551341

18 • A1 | Tillamook SF - South Fork Trask

Total sites: 2, RV sites: 2, No water, No toilets, Tent & RV camping: Free, Elev: 1699ft/518m, Tel: 503-842-2545, Nearest town: Tillamook. GPS: 45.371816, -123.596855

19 • A1 | Tillamook SF - Stagecoach Horse Camp

Total sites: 9, RV sites: 9, No water, Vault/pit toilet, Tent & RV camping: $20, Horses-only in summer, Stock water, Open all year, Max Length: 25ft, Reservations not accepted, Elev: 1978ft/603m, Tel: 503-357-2191, Nearest town: Tillamook. GPS: 45.602161, -123.412721

20 • A2 | Tillamook SF - Browns OHV Camp

Total sites: 29, RV sites: 29, Central water, Vault/pit toilet, No showers, No RV dump, Tent & RV camping: $20, 1 group site $50, Open Apr-Oct, Max Length: 40ft, Reservations not accepted, Elev: 1562ft/476m, Tel: 503-357-2191, Nearest town: Forest Grove. GPS: 45.610854, -123.348821

21 • A2 | Tillamook SF - Gales Creek

Total sites: 21, RV sites: 17, Central water, Vault/pit toilet, No showers, No RV dump, Tents: $15/RVs: $20, Also walk-to sites, 4 walk-to sites, Open May-Sep, Reservations not accepted, Elev: 991ft/302m, Tel: 503-357-2191, Nearest town: Tillamook. GPS: 45.643181, -123.358703

22 • A2 | Tillamook SF - Reehers Horse Camp

Total sites: 17, RV sites: 17, Central water, Vault/pit toilet, Tent & RV camping: $20, 10 corral sites, Open May-Sep, Reservations not accepted, Elev: 1207ft/368m, Tel: 503-357-2191, Nearest town: Tillamook. GPS: 45.706354, -123.333571

23 • B2 | Santiam SF - Butte Creek Falls

Total sites: 3, RV sites: 3, No water, Vault/pit toilet, Tent & RV camping: $20, Open May-Sep, Reservations not accepted, Elev: 2046ft/624m, Tel: 503-859-2151, Nearest town: Lyons. GPS: 44.921058, -122.511583

24 • B2 | Santiam SF - Horse Camp

Total sites: 12, RV sites: 10, No water, Vault/pit toilet, Tents: $15/RVs: $20, Open May-Sep, Reservations not accepted, Elev: 1676ft/511m, Tel: 503-859-2151, Nearest town: Gates. GPS: 44.730093, -122.402693

25 • B2 | Santiam SF - Rhody Lake

Total sites: 3, RV sites: 3, No water, Vault/pit toilet, Tent & RV camping: Free, Open May-Sep, Reservations not accepted, Elev: 3674ft/1120m, Tel: 503-859-2151, Nearest town: Lyons. GPS: 44.892227, -122.409657

26 • B2 | Santiam SF - Shellburg Falls

Total sites: 7, RV sites: 4, Central water, Vault/pit toilet, Tents: $15/RVs: $20, Open May-Oct, Reservations not accepted, Elev: 1471ft/448m, Tel: 503-859-2151, Nearest town: Lyons. GPS: 44.816463, -122.610888

27 • B4 | Ukiah-Dale Forest State Scenic Corridor

Total sites: 27, RV sites: 27, Central water, Flush toilet, No showers, No RV dump, Tent & RV camping: $10, Open Apr-Oct, Max Length: 40ft, Reservations not accepted, Elev: 3300ft/1006m, Tel: 800-551-6949, Nearest town: Ukiah. GPS: 45.124603, -118.972458

28 • C1 | Brown's OHV Camp - SF

Total sites: 29, RV sites: 29, Central water, Vault/pit toilet, No showers, No RV dump, Tent & RV camping: $20, 1 group site $50, Open Apr-Oct, Reservations not accepted, Elev: 702ft/214m, Tel: 503-357-2191, Nearest town: Tillamook. GPS: 43.610063, -123.351225

Pennsylvania

Map	ID	Map	ID
B5	1-7	D3	9
D2	8		

Alphabetical List of Camping Areas

Name	ID	Map
Buchanan SF	9	D3
Delaware SF - Bridge Camp (E-8)	1	B5
Delaware SF - CCC Camp (E-13)	2	B5
Delaware SF - Laurel Run (S-3)	3	B5
Delaware SF - Lily Pond (O-30)	4	B5
Delaware SF - Maple Run (E-11)	5	B5
Delaware SF - Middle Branch (E-7)	6	B5
Delaware SF - Shanty Draft (S-4)	7	B5
Forbes SF	8	D2

1 • B5 | Delaware SF - Bridge Camp (E-8)

Dispersed sites, No water, No toilets, Tent & RV camping: Free, Free permit required, Reservations required, Elev: 1270ft/387m, Tel: 570-895-4000, Nearest town: Lords Valley. GPS: 41.231286, -75.109336

2 • B5 | Delaware SF - CCC Camp (E-13)

Dispersed sites, No water, No toilets, Tent & RV camping: Free, Free permit required, Max Length: 20ft, Reservations not accepted, Elev: 1345ft/410m, Tel: 570-895-4000, Nearest town: Dingmans Ferry. GPS: 41.257522, -74.992237

3 • B5 | Delaware SF - Laurel Run (S-3)

Dispersed sites, No water, No toilets, Tent & RV camping: Free, Nothing larger than van/PU, Free permit required, Reservations required, Elev: 1088ft/332m, Tel: 570-895-4000, Nearest town: Stroudsburg. GPS: 41.135303, -75.210617

4 • B5 | Delaware SF - Lily Pond (O-30)

Dispersed sites, No water, No toilets, Tent & RV camping: Free, Free permit required, Reservations required, Elev: 1158ft/353m, Tel: 570-895-4000, Nearest town: Milford. GPS: 41.359964, -74.854999

5 • B5 | Delaware SF - Maple Run (E-11)

Dispersed sites, No water, No toilets, Tent & RV camping: Free, Free permit required, Reservations required, Elev: 1500ft/457m, Tel: 570-895-4000, Nearest town: Lords Valley. GPS: 41.304787, -75.100966

6 • B5 | Delaware SF - Middle Branch (E-7)

Dispersed sites, No water, No toilets, Tent & RV camping: Free, Nothing larger than van/PU, Free permit required, Reservations required, Elev: 1262ft/385m, Tel: 570-895-4000, Nearest town: Lords Valley. GPS: 41.235202, -75.106485

7 • B5 | Delaware SF - Shanty Draft (S-4)

Dispersed sites, No water, No toilets, Tent & RV camping: Free, Free permit required, Reservations required, Elev: 1048ft/319m, Tel: 570-895-4000, Nearest town: Stroudsburg. GPS: 41.132053, -75.213547

8 • D2 | Forbes SF

Dispersed sites, No water, No toilets, Tent & RV camping: Free, Reservations not accepted, Elev: 2691ft/820m, Nearest town: Somerset. GPS: 40.130435, -79.181826

9 • D3 | Buchanan SF

Dispersed sites, No water, No toilets, Tent & RV camping: Free, Free permit required, Reservations not accepted, Elev: 2201ft/671m, Tel: 717-485-3148, Nearest town: Chambersburg. GPS: 40.015185, -78.151696

Tennessee

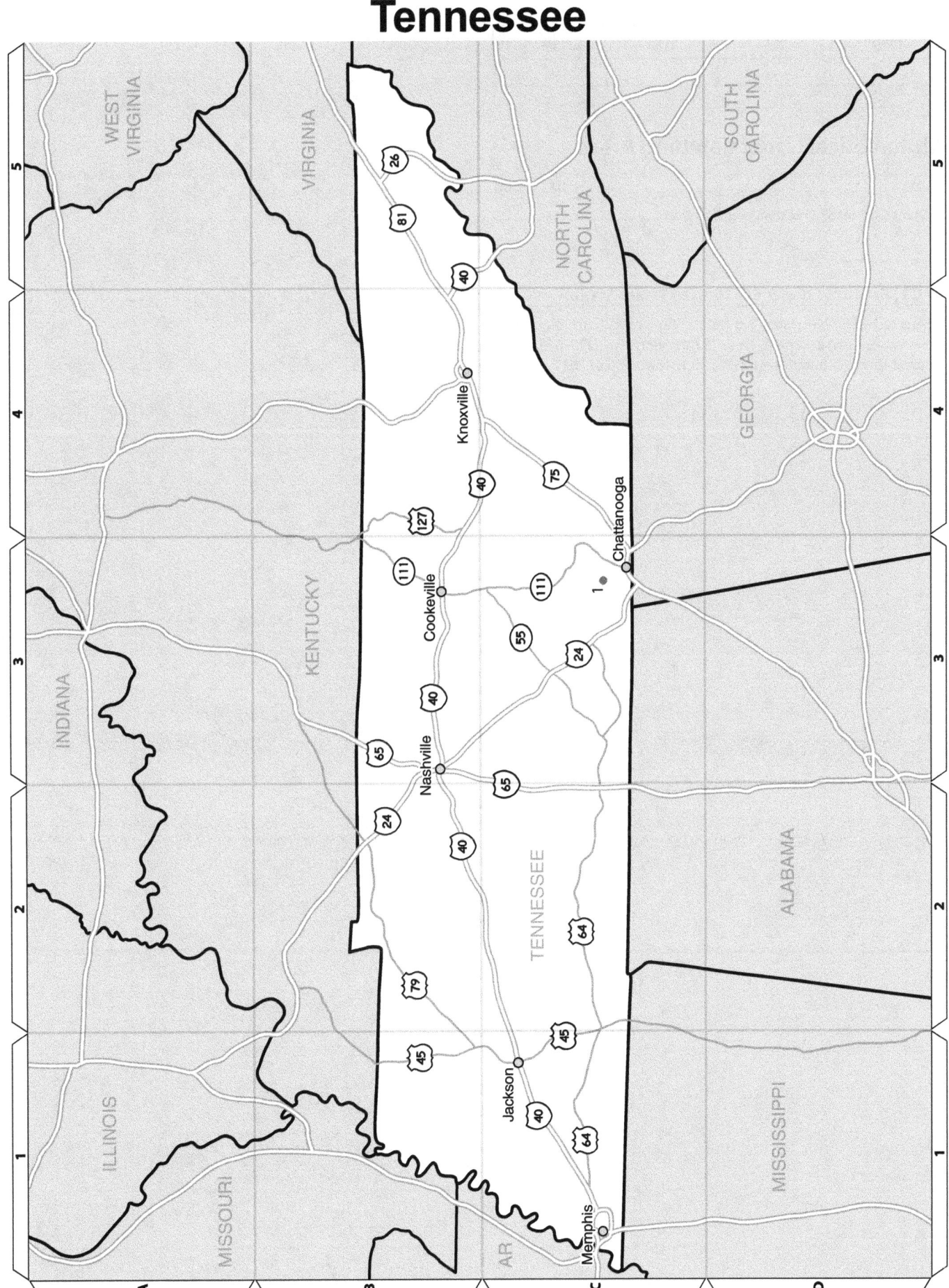

Map	ID	Map	ID
C3	1		

Alphabetical List of Camping Areas

Name   **ID**   **Map**

Prentice Cooper SF - Hunters Check Station .... 1 .... C3

1 • C3 | Prentice Cooper SF - Hunters Check Station

Dispersed sites, No water, No toilets, Tent & RV camping: Free, Reservations not accepted, Elev: 1923ft/586m, Tel: 423-658-5551, Nearest town: Chattanooga. GPS: 35.164342, -85.417017

Washington

Map	ID	Map	ID
A2	1	B5	29-30
A4	2-10	C1	31-34
A5	11-17	C2	36-40
B1	18-23	C3	41-48
B2	24-27	D2	49-50
B3	28	D3	51-52

Alphabetical List of Camping Areas

Name	ID	Map
Ahtanum SF - Ahtanum	41	C3
Ahtanum SF - Ahtanum Meadows	42	C3
Ahtanum SF - BBQ Flats	43	C3
Ahtanum SF - Bird Creek	51	D3
Ahtanum SF - Clover Flats	44	C3
Ahtanum SF - Island Camp	52	D3
Ahtanum SF - Snow Cabin	45	C3
Ahtanum SF - Tree Phones Horse Camp	46	C3
Coppermine Bottom - DNR	18	B1
Cottonwood - DNR	19	B1
Elbe Hills SF - Elbe Hills ORV	35	C2
Elbe Hills SF - Sahara Creek Horse Camp	36	C2
Fall Creek - DNR	37	C2
Green Mt SF - Horse Camp	24	B2
Hoh Oxbow - DNR	20	B1
Les Hilde TH - DNR	1	A2
Little Pend Oreille SF - Douglas Falls Grange Park	11	A5
Little Pend Oreille SF - Dragoon Creek	29	B5
Little Pend Oreille SF - Flodelle Creek	12	A5
Little Pend Oreille SF - Rocky Lake	13	A5
Little Pend Oreille SF - Sheep Creek	14	A5
Little Pend Oreille SF - Sherry Creek	15	A5
Little Pend Oreille SF - Skookum Creek	30	B5
Little Pend Oreille SF - Starvation Lake	16	A5
Little Pend Oreille SF - Upper Sheep Creek	17	A5
Loomis SF - Chopaka Lake	2	A4
Loomis SF - Cold Springs	3	A4
Loomis SF - North Fork Nine Mile	4	A4
Loomis SF - Palmer Lake	5	A4
Loomis SF - Toats Coulee	6	A4
Loup Loup SF - Leader Lake	7	A4
Loup Loup SF - Rock Creek	8	A4
Loup Loup SF - Rock Lakes	9	A4
Loup Loup SF - Sportsman's Camp	10	A4
Lyre River - DNR	21	B1
Margaret McKenny - DNR	38	C2
Middle Waddell - DNR	39	C2
Minnie Peterson - DNR	22	B1
Porter Creek - DNR	31	C1
South Fork Hoh - DNR	23	B1
Tahuya SF - Camp Spilman - DNR	25	B2
Tahuya SF - Kammenga Canyon	26	B2
Tahuya SF - Tahuya River Horse Camp	27	B2
Teanaway SF - 29 Pines	28	B3
Teanaway SF - Indian Camp	47	C3
Teanaway SF - Teanaway	48	C3
Yacolt Burn SF - Cold Creek	49	D2
Yacolt Burn SF - Dougan Creek	50	D2
Yacolt Burn SF - Snag Lake	32	C1
Yacolt Burn SF - Tunerville Horse Camp	33	C1
Yacolt Burn SF - Western Lake	34	C1
Yacolt Burn SF - Winston Creek	40	C2

1 • A2 | Les Hilde TH - DNR

Dispersed sites, No water, Vault/pit toilet, Tent & RV camping: $10, Discover Pass ($10/day or $30/year) required, Elev: 381ft/116m. GPS: 48.544621, -121.985497

2 • A4 | Loomis SF - Chopaka Lake

Total sites: 16, RV sites: 16, Central water, Vault/pit toilet, No showers, No RV dump, Tent & RV camping: $10, Road may be inaccessible in winter, Discover Pass ($10/day or $30/year) required, Stay limit: 7 days, Max Length: 20ft, Reservations not accepted, Elev: 2913ft/888m, Tel: 509-684-7474, Nearest town: Tonasket. GPS: 48.913622, -119.702079

3 • A4 | Loomis SF - Cold Springs

Total sites: 5, RV sites: 5, No water, Vault/pit toilet, Tent & RV camping: $10, Discover Pass ($10/day or $30/year) required, Stay limit: 7 days, Reservations not accepted, Elev: 2545ft/776m, Tel: 509-684-7474, Nearest town: Loomis. GPS: 48.843225, -119.714263

4 • A4 | Loomis SF - North Fork Nine Mile

Total sites: 11, RV sites: 11, Central water, Vault/pit toilet, Tent & RV camping: $10, Discover Pass ($10/day or $30/year) required, Stay limit: 7 days, Reservations not accepted, Elev: 3560ft/1085m, Tel: 509-684-7474. GPS: 48.866654, -119.770566

5 • A4 | Loomis SF - Palmer Lake

Total sites: 7, RV sites: 7, No water, Vault/pit toilet, Tent & RV camping: $10, Discover Pass ($10/day or $30/year) required, Stay limit: 7 days, Reservations not accepted, Elev: 1266ft/386m, Tel: 509-684-7474, Nearest town: Loomis. GPS: 48.915762, -119.637126

6 • A4 | Loomis SF - Toats Coulee

Total sites: 9, RV sites: 9, No water, Vault/pit toilet, Tent & RV camping: $10, Discover Pass ($10/day or $30/year) required, Stay limit: 7 days, Reservations not accepted, Elev: 2686ft/819m, Tel: 509-684-7474, Nearest town: Tonasket. GPS: 48.849394, -119.735966

7 • A4 | Loup Loup SF - Leader Lake

Total sites: 16, RV sites: 16, No water, Vault/pit toilet, Tent & RV camping: $10, Discover Pass ($10/day or $30/year) required, Reservations not accepted, Elev: 2303ft/702m, Tel: 509-684-7474, Nearest town: Okanogan. GPS: 48.362054, -119.695346

8 • A4 | Loup Loup SF - Rock Creek

Total sites: 19, RV sites: 19, No water, Vault/pit toilet, Tent & RV camping: $10, Discover Pass ($10/day or $30/year) required, Reservations not accepted, Elev: 2445ft/745m, Tel: 509-684-7474, Nearest town: Okanogan. GPS: 48.406283, -119.758806

9 • A4 | Loup Loup SF - Rock Lakes

Total sites: 8, RV sites: 8, No water, Vault/pit toilet, Tent & RV camping: $10, Discover Pass ($10/day or $30/year) required, Reservations not accepted, Elev: 3824ft/1166m, Tel: 509-684-7474, Nearest town: Okanogan. GPS: 48.453317, -119.787677

10 • A4 | Loup Loup SF - Sportsman's Camp

Total sites: 6, RV sites: 6, No water, Vault/pit toilet, Tent & RV camping: $10, Discover Pass ($10/day or $30/year) required, Reservations not accepted, Elev: 3254ft/992m, Tel: 509-684-7474, Nearest town: Okanogan. GPS: 48.391661, -119.807924

11 • A5 | Little Pend Oreille SF - Douglas Falls Grange Park

Total sites: 9, RV sites: 9, Central water, Vault/pit toilet, No showers, No RV dump, Tent & RV camping: $10, Discover Pass ($10/day or $30/year) required, Reservations not accepted, Elev: 1942ft/592m, Tel: 509-684-7474, Nearest town: Colville. GPS: 48.615038, -117.896704

12 • A5 | Little Pend Oreille SF - Flodelle Creek

Total sites: 8, RV sites: 8, Central water, Vault/pit toilet, No showers, No RV dump, Tent & RV camping: $10, Discover Pass ($10/day or $30/year) required, Reservations not accepted, Elev: 3120ft/951m, Tel: 509-684-7474, Nearest town: Colville. GPS: 48.544976, -117.572736

13 • A5 | Little Pend Oreille SF - Rocky Lake

Total sites: 5, RV sites: 5, Central water, Vault/pit toilet, No showers, No RV dump, Tent & RV camping: $10, Discover Pass ($10/day or $30/year) required, Open Apr-Oct, Reservations not accepted, Elev: 2244ft/684m, Tel: 509-684-7474, Nearest town: Colville. GPS: 48.495986, -117.871943

14 • A5 | Little Pend Oreille SF - Sheep Creek

Total sites: 12, RV sites: 12, Central water, Vault/pit toilet, No showers, No RV dump, Tent & RV camping: $10, Discover Pass ($10/day or $30/year) required, Reservations not accepted, Elev: 2008ft/612m, Tel: 509-684-7474, Nearest town: Northport. GPS: 48.959882, -117.834471

15 • A5 | Little Pend Oreille SF - Sherry Creek

Total sites: 7, RV sites: 7, No water, Vault/pit toilet, Tent & RV camping: $10, Discover Pass ($10/day or $30/year) required, Reservations not accepted, Elev: 3205ft/977m, Tel: 509-684-7474, Nearest town: Colville. GPS: 48.604826, -117.541956

16 • A5 | Little Pend Oreille SF - Starvation Lake

Total sites: 12, RV sites: 12, No water, Vault/pit toilet, Tent & RV camping: $10, Discover Pass ($10/day or $30/year) required, Reservations not accepted, Elev: 2431ft/741m, Tel: 509-684-7474, Nearest town: Colville. GPS: 48.492587, -117.709289

17 • A5 | Little Pend Oreille SF - Upper Sheep Creek

Total sites: 2, RV sites: 2, No water, Vault/pit toilet, Tent & RV camping: $10, Discover Pass ($10/day or $30/year) required, Reservations not accepted, Elev: 2007ft/612m, Tel: 509-684-7474, Nearest town: Northport. GPS: 48.960629, -117.856503

18 • B1 | Coppermine Bottom - DNR

Total sites: 11, RV sites: 11, No water, Vault/pit toilet, Tent & RV camping: $10, Discover Pass ($10/day or $30/year) required, Generator hours: 0600-2200, Open all year, Reservations not accepted, Elev: 276ft/84m, Tel: 360-374-2800, Nearest town: Forks. GPS: 47.656405, -124.198994

19 • B1 | Cottonwood - DNR

Total sites: 9, RV sites: 9, No water, Vault/pit toilet, Tent & RV camping: $10, Discover Pass ($10/day or $30/year) required, Generator hours: 0600-2200, Open all year, Reservations not accepted, Elev: 187ft/57m, Tel: 360-374-2800, Nearest town: Forks. GPS: 47.777499, -124.292937

20 • B1 | Hoh Oxbow - DNR

Total sites: 8, RV sites: 8, No water, Vault/pit toilet, Tent & RV camping: $10, Discover Pass ($10/day or $30/year) required, Generator hours: 0600-2200, Open all year, Reservations not accepted, Elev: 282ft/86m, Tel: 360-374-2800, Nearest town: Aberdeen. GPS: 47.809795, -124.249441

21 • B1 | Lyre River - DNR

Total sites: 11, RV sites: 11, Central water, Vault/pit toilet, No showers, No RV dump, Tent & RV camping: $10, Discover Pass ($10/day or $30/year) required, Stay limit: 7 days, Generator hours: 0600-2200, Open all year, Max Length: 20ft, Reservations not accepted, Elev: 134ft/41m, Tel: 360-374-6131, Nearest town: Port Angeles. GPS: 48.151655, -123.831885

22 • B1 | Minnie Peterson - DNR

Total sites: 9, RV sites: 9, Central water, Vault/pit toilet, No showers, No RV dump, Tent & RV camping: $10, Discover Pass ($10/day or $30/year) required, Generator hours: 0600-2200, Open all year, Max Length: 22ft, Reservations not accepted, Elev: 413ft/126m, Tel: 360-374-2800, Nearest town: Forks. GPS: 47.819160, -124.175690

23 • B1 | South Fork Hoh - DNR

Total sites: 3, RV sites: 3, No water, Vault/pit toilet, Tent & RV camping: $10, Discover Pass ($10/day or $30/year) required, Generator hours: 0600-2200, Open all year, Reservations not accepted, Elev: 571ft/174m, Tel: 360-374-2800, Nearest town: Forks. GPS: 47.806252, -123.995648

24 • B2 | Green Mt SF - Horse Camp

Total sites: 12, RV sites: 12, No water, Vault/pit toilet, Tent & RV camping: $10, Discover Pass ($10/day or $30/year) required, Reservations not accepted, Elev: 1174ft/358m, Tel: 360-825-1631, Nearest town: Silverdale. GPS: 47.578683, -122.792167

25 • B2 | Tahuya SF - Camp Spilman - DNR

Total sites: 11, RV sites: 11, No water, Vault/pit toilet, Tent & RV camping: $10, Discover Pass ($10/day or $30/year) required, Stay limit: 7 days, Open all year, Max Length: 30ft, Reservations not accepted, Elev: 322ft/98m, Tel: 360-825-1631, Nearest town: Belfair. GPS: 47.476624, -122.926711

26 • B2 | Tahuya SF - Kammenga Canyon

Total sites: 6, RV sites: 6, No water, Vault/pit toilet, Tent & RV camping: $10, Discover Pass ($10/day or $30/year) required, Stay limit: 7 days, Reservations not accepted, Elev: 337ft/103m,

Tel: 360-825-1631, Nearest town: Belfair. GPS: 47.479993, -122.918998

27 • B2 | Tahuya SF - Tahuya River Horse Camp

Total sites: 10, RV sites: 10, Tent & RV camping: $10, Discover Pass ($10/day or $30/year) required, Open weekends - camping allowed weekdays, Stay limit: 7 days, Open Apr-Oct, Reservations not accepted, Elev: 292ft/89m, Tel: 360-825-1631, Nearest town: Belfair. GPS: 47.467416, -122.942382

28 • B3 | Teanaway SF - 29 Pines

Total sites: 59, RV sites: 59, No water, Vault/pit toilet, Tent & RV camping: $10, No campfires, Discover Pass ($10/day or $30/year) required, Reservations not accepted, Elev: 2603ft/793m, Tel: 509-925-8510, Nearest town: Cle Elum. GPS: 47.328779, -120.854347

29 • B5 | Little Pend Oreille SF - Dragoon Creek

Total sites: 22, RV sites: 22, Central water, Vault/pit toilet, No showers, No RV dump, Tent & RV camping: $10, No pets, Discover Pass ($10/day or $30/year) required, Reservations not accepted, Elev: 1968ft/600m, Tel: 509-684-7474, Nearest town: Spokane. GPS: 47.888354, -117.443023

30 • B5 | Little Pend Oreille SF - Skookum Creek

Total sites: 10, RV sites: 10, Central water, Vault/pit toilet, No showers, No RV dump, Tent & RV camping: $10, Discover Pass ($10/day or $30/year) required, Reservations not accepted, Elev: 2059ft/628m, Tel: 509-684-7474, Nearest town: Usk. GPS: 48.292429, -117.226773

31 • C1 | Porter Creek - DNR

Total sites: 16, RV sites: 16, Central water, Vault/pit toilet, No showers, No RV dump, Tent & RV camping: $10, Discover Pass ($10/day or $30/year) required, Open May-Nov, Reservations not accepted, Elev: 486ft/148m, Tel: 360-825-1631, Nearest town: Porter. GPS: 46.977998, -123.255451

32 • C1 | Yacolt Burn SF - Snag Lake

Total sites: 5, RV sites: 5, No water, Vault/pit toilet, Tent & RV camping: $10, Discover Pass ($10/day or $30/year) required, Reservations not accepted, Elev: 1112ft/339m, Tel: 360-577-2025, Nearest town: Naselle. GPS: 46.423728, -123.821822

33 • C1 | Yacolt Burn SF - Tunerville Horse Camp

Total sites: 4, RV sites: 4, No water, Vault/pit toilet, Tent & RV camping: $10, 2 corrals, Discover Pass ($10/day or $30/year) required, Reservations not accepted, Elev: 430ft/131m, Tel: 360-577-2025, Nearest town: Rosburg. GPS: 46.407367, -123.627031

34 • C1 | Yacolt Burn SF - Western Lake

Total sites: 3, RV sites: 3, No water, Vault/pit toilet, Tent & RV camping: $10, Discover Pass ($10/day or $30/year) required, Reservations not accepted, Elev: 1260ft/384m, Tel: 360-577-2025, Nearest town: Naselle. GPS: 46.419888, -123.815178

35 • C2 | Elbe Hills SF - Elbe Hills ORV

Total sites: 25, RV sites: 15, No water, Vault/pit toilet, Tent & RV camping: $10, Discover Pass ($10/day or $30/year) required, Reservations required, Elev: 1982ft/604m, Tel: 360-825-1631, Nearest town: Ashford. GPS: 46.768918, -122.079595

36 • C2 | Elbe Hills SF - Sahara Creek Horse Camp

Total sites: 20, RV sites: 20, Central water, Vault/pit toilet, Tent & RV camping: $10, Discover Pass ($10/day or $30/year) required, Reservations not accepted, Elev: 1565ft/477m, Tel: 360-825-1631, Nearest town: Ashford. GPS: 46.758411, -122.085778

37 • C2 | Fall Creek - DNR

Total sites: 8, RV sites: 8, Central water, Vault/pit toilet, No showers, No RV dump, Tent & RV camping: $10, Discover Pass ($10/day or $30/year) required, Corral, Open May-Nov, Elev: 715ft/218m, Tel: 360-825-1631, Nearest town: Littlerock. GPS: 46.940471, -123.128886

38 • C2 | Margaret McKenny - DNR

Total sites: 24, RV sites: 24, Central water, Vault/pit toilet, No showers, No RV dump, Tent & RV camping: $10, Corrals, Discover Pass ($10/day or $30/year) required, Open May-Nov, Elev: 368ft/112m, Tel: 800-527-3305, Nearest town: Littlerock. GPS: 46.925845, -123.059532

39 • C2 | Middle Waddell - DNR

Total sites: 24, RV sites: 24, Central water, Vault/pit toilet, No showers, No RV dump, Tent & RV camping: $10, Discover Pass ($10/day or $30/year) required, Open May-Nov, Elev: 351ft/107m, Tel: 800-527-3305, Nearest town: Littlerock. GPS: 46.939125, -123.075304

40 • C2 | Yacolt Burn SF - Winston Creek

Total sites: 12, RV sites: 12, Vault/pit toilet, Tent & RV camping: $10, Discover Pass ($10/day or $30/year) required, Open Apr-Dec, Reservations not accepted, Elev: 696ft/212m, Tel: 360-577-2025, Nearest town: Salkum. GPS: 46.479794, -122.505006

41 • C3 | Ahtanum SF - Ahtanum

Total sites: 12, RV sites: 12, Central water, Vault/pit toilet, Tent & RV camping: $10, Discover Pass ($10/day or $30/year) required, Sno-Park permit required if camping between 11/01 and 05/01, Open May-Sep, Reservations not accepted, Elev: 3235ft/986m, Tel: 509-925-8510, Nearest town: Yakima. GPS: 46.510677, -121.020346

42 • C3 | Ahtanum SF - Ahtanum Meadows

Total sites: 10, RV sites: 10, Vault/pit toilet, Tent & RV camping: $10, Discover Pass ($10/day or $30/year) required, Reservations not accepted, Elev: 3104ft/946m, Tel: 509-925-8510, Nearest town: Yakima. GPS: 46.519896, -121.013087

43 • C3 | Ahtanum SF - BBQ Flats

Dispersed sites, No water, Vault/pit toilet, Tent & RV camping: $10, Discover Pass ($10/day or $30/year) required, Reservations not accepted, Elev: 3497ft/1066m, Tel: 509-925-8519, Nearest town: Nile. GPS: 46.868731, -120.811582

44 • C3 | Ahtanum SF - Clover Flats

Total sites: 9, RV sites: 9, Central water, Vault/pit toilet, No showers, No RV dump, Tent & RV camping: $10, Very steep road, Discover Pass ($10/day or $30/year) required, Reservations not accepted, Elev: 6280ft/1914m, Tel: 509-925-8510, Nearest town: Yakima. GPS: 46.507174, -121.176804

45 • C3 | Ahtanum SF - Snow Cabin

Total sites: 8, RV sites: 8, No water, Vault/pit toilet, Tent & RV camping: $10, Discover Pass ($10/day or $30/year) required, Reservations not accepted, Elev: 4580ft/1396m, Tel: 509-925-8510, Nearest town: Yakima. GPS: 46.530241, -121.152432

46 • C3 | Ahtanum SF - Tree Phones Horse Camp

Total sites: 14, RV sites: 14, Central water, Vault/pit toilet, No showers, No RV dump, Tent & RV camping: $10, Hitching posts, Discover Pass ($10/day or $30/year) required, Reservations not accepted, Elev: 4837ft/1474m, Tel: 509-925-8510, Nearest town: Yakima. GPS: 46.497871, -121.120722

47 • C3 | Teanaway SF - Indian Camp

Total sites: 11, RV sites: 11, No water, Vault/pit toilet, Tent & RV camping: $10, 2 group sites, Discover Pass ($10/day or $30/year) required, Reservations not accepted, Elev: 2654ft/809m, Tel: 509-925-8510, Nearest town: Cle Elum. GPS: 47.290352, -120.955199

48 • C3 | Teanaway SF - Teanaway

Total sites: 64, RV sites: 64, No water, Vault/pit toilet, Tent & RV camping: $10, Discover Pass ($10/day or $30/year) required, Reservations not accepted, Elev: 2262ft/689m, Tel: 509-925-8510, Nearest town: Cle Elum. GPS: 47.256815, -120.892711

49 • D2 | Yacolt Burn SF - Cold Creek

Total sites: 8, RV sites: 8, No water, Vault/pit toilet, No showers, No RV dump, Tent & RV camping: $10, Discover Pass ($10/day or $30/year) required, Reservations not accepted, Elev: 1168ft/356m, Tel: 360-577-2025, Nearest town: Hockinson. GPS: 45.761707, -122.339877

50 • D2 | Yacolt Burn SF - Dougan Creek

Total sites: 7, RV sites: 7, No water, Vault/pit toilet, Tent & RV camping: $10, Discover Pass ($10/day or $30/year) required, Open May-Nov, Reservations not accepted, Elev: 647ft/197m, Tel: 360-577-2025, Nearest town: North Bonneville. GPS: 45.672919, -122.154182

51 • D3 | Ahtanum SF - Bird Creek

Total sites: 9, RV sites: 9, No water, Vault/pit toilet, Tent & RV camping: $10, Discover Pass ($10/day or $30/year) required, Reservations not accepted, Elev: 2634ft/803m, Tel: 509-925-8510, Nearest town: Glenwood. GPS: 46.062746, -121.337435

52 • D3 | Ahtanum SF - Island Camp

Total sites: 6, RV sites: 6, No water, Vault/pit toilet, Tent & RV camping: $10, Discover Pass ($10/day or $30/year) required, Reservations not accepted, Elev: 3410ft/1039m, Tel: 509-925-8510, Nearest town: Glenwood. GPS: 46.081114, -121.380033

West Virginia

Map	ID	Map	ID
B3	1	C3	5-6
C1	2-4	D3	7

Alphabetical List of Camping Areas

Name	ID	Map
Cabwaylingo SF - Spruce Creek	2	C1
Cabwaylingo SF - Tick Ridge	3	C1
Coopers Rock SF - McCollum	1	B3
Greenbrier SF	7	D3
Kanawha SF	4	C2
Kumbrabow SF	5	C3
Seneca SF	6	C3

1 • B3 | Coopers Rock SF - McCollum

Total sites: 25, RV sites: 25, Elec sites: 25, Central water, Flush toilet, Free showers, No RV dump, Tent & RV camping: $31, Stay limit: 14 days, Open Apr-Oct, Reservations accepted, Elev: 2116ft/645m, Tel: 304-594-1561, Nearest town: Morgantown. GPS: 39.640497, -79.792104

2 • C1 | Cabwaylingo SF - Spruce Creek

Total sites: 11, RV sites: 11, Elec sites: 6, Water at site, Flush toilet, Free showers, Tents: $23-28/RVs: $28-33, Stay limit: 14 days, Open Apr-Oct, Reservations accepted, Elev: 869ft/265m, Tel: 304-385-4255, Nearest town: Dunlow. GPS: 37.966776, -82.356674

3 • C1 | Cabwaylingo SF - Tick Ridge

Total sites: 8, RV sites: 8, Central water, Vault/pit toilet, No showers, No RV dump, Tent & RV camping: $16, Stay limit: 14 days, Open Apr-Oct, Reservations not accepted, Elev: 1224ft/373m, Tel: 304-385-4255, Nearest town: Dunlow. GPS: 37.980238, -82.389023

4 • C2 | Kanawha SF

Total sites: 46, RV sites: 46, Elec sites: 25, Water at site, Flush toilet, Free showers, RV dump, Tents: $27/RVs: $33, Stay limit: 14 days, Open Apr-Dec, Reservations accepted, Elev: 1030ft/314m, Tel: 304-558-3500, Nearest town: Charleston. GPS: 38.252799, -81.661502

5 • C3 | Kumbrabow SF

Total sites: 12, RV sites: 12, Central water, Vault/pit toilet, Pay showers, No RV dump, Tent & RV camping: $16, Also cabins, Stay limit: 14 days, Open Apr-Nov, Max Length: 60ft, Reservations accepted, Elev: 3140ft/957m, Tel: 304-335-2219, Nearest town: Huttonsville. GPS: 38.644986, -80.080024

6 • C3 | Seneca SF

Total sites: 10, RV sites: 10, Central water, Flush toilet, Pay showers, No RV dump, Tent & RV camping: $20, Also cabins, Group site: $60, Stay limit: 14 days, Open Apr-Nov, Reservations not accepted, Elev: 2746ft/837m, Tel: 304-799-6213, Nearest town: Dunmore. GPS: 38.306923, -79.921317

7 • D3 | Greenbrier SF

Total sites: 16, RV sites: 16, Elec sites: 16, Central water, Flush toilet, Free showers, No RV dump, Tent & RV camping: $32, Also cabins, Stay limit: 14 days, Open Apr-Oct, Reservations accepted, Elev: 1978ft/603m, Tel: 304-536-1944, Nearest town: Caldwell. GPS: 37.729505, -80.363141

Wisconsin

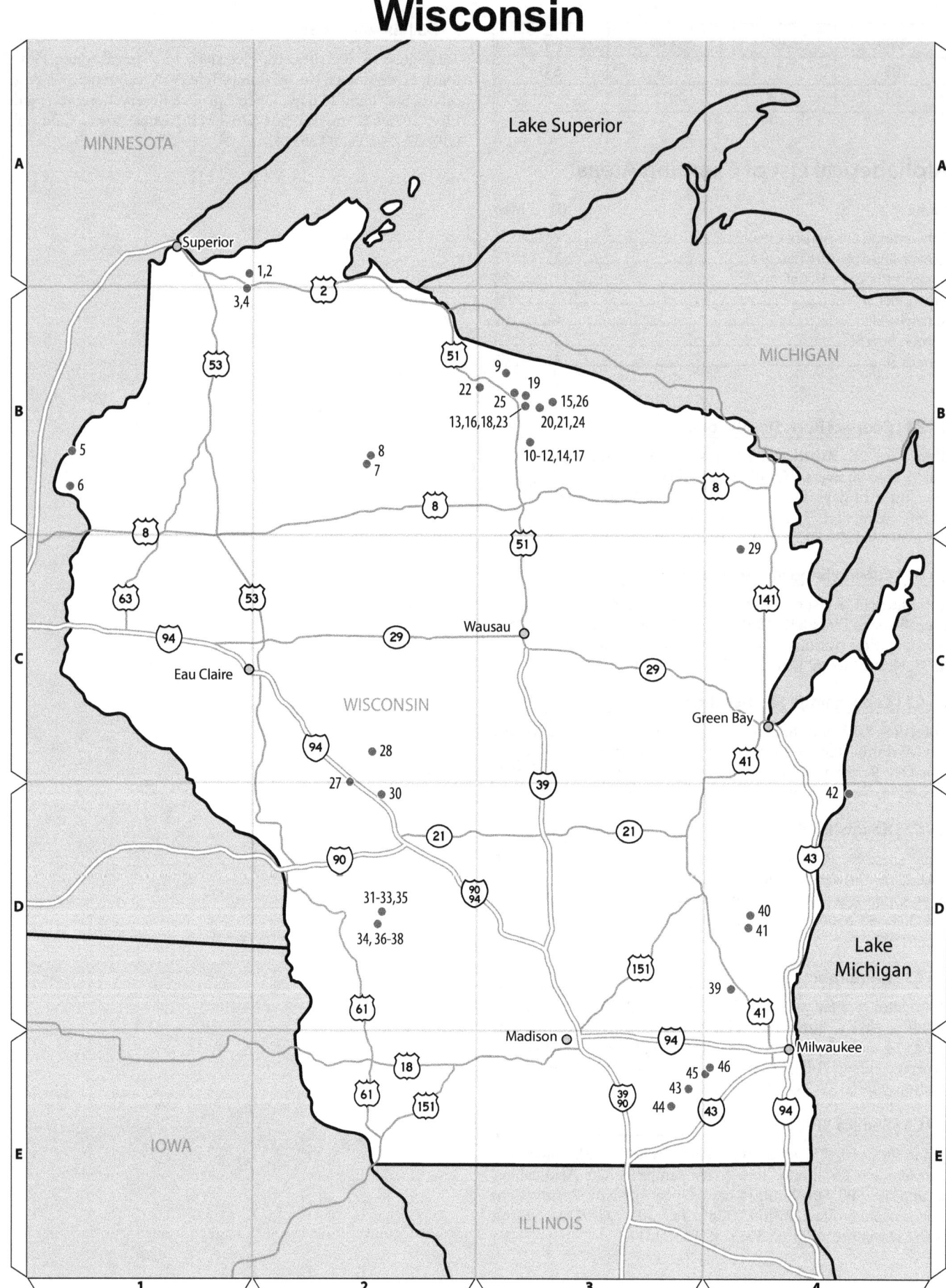

Map	ID	Map	ID
A1	1-2	C4	29
B1	3-6	D2	30-38
B2	7-8	D4	39-42
B3	9-26	E3	43-44
C2	27-28	E4	45-46

Alphabetical List of Camping Areas

Name	ID	Map
Black River SF - Castle Mound CG	27	C2
Black River SF - East Fork CG	28	C2
Black River SF - Pigeon Creek CG	30	D2
Bois Brule - Brule River SF	3	B1
Brule River SF - Bois Brule	4	B1
Brule River SF - Copper Range	1	A1
Copper Range - Brule River SF	2	A1
Flambeau River SF - Connor Lake	7	B2
Flambeau River SF - Lake Of The Pines	8	B2
Governor Knowles SF - St Croix	5	B1
Governor Knowles SF - Trade River Horse Camp	6	B1
Kettle Moraine SF - Pike Lake Unit	39	D4
Kettle-Moraine SF - Horseriders	43	E3
Kettle-Moraine SF - Ottawa Lake	45	E4
Kettle-Moraine SF - Pinewoods	46	E4
Kettle-Moraine SF - Whitewater	44	E3
Kickapoo Valley Reserve - Bare Beach - KRMB	31	D2
Kickapoo Valley Reserve - Bridge Seven - KRMB	32	D2
Kickapoo Valley Reserve - Cutoff Camp	33	D2
Kickapoo Valley Reserve - Daines Valley - KRMB	34	D2
Kickapoo Valley Reserve - Hay Valley - KRMB	35	D2
Kickapoo Valley Reserve - Jug Creek	36	D2
Kickapoo Valley Reserve - Mule Camp - KRMB	37	D2
Kickapoo Valley Reserve - Potts Corners - KRMB	38	D2
Long Lake - Kettle-Moraine SF	40	D4
Mauthe Lake - Kettle-Moraine SF	41	D4
Northern Highland-American Legion SF - Big Lake	9	B3
Northern Highland-American Legion SF - Buffalo Lake	10	B3
Northern Highland-American Legion SF - Carrol Lake	11	B3
Northern Highland-American Legion SF - Clear Lake	12	B3
Northern Highland-American Legion SF - Crystal Lake	13	B3
Northern Highland-American Legion SF - Cunard Lake	14	B3
Northern Highland-American Legion SF - East Star Lake	15	B3
Northern Highland-American Legion SF - Firefly Lake	16	B3
Northern Highland-American Legion SF - Indian Mounds	17	B3
Northern Highland-American Legion SF - Musky Lake	18	B3
Northern Highland-American Legion SF - North Trout Lake	19	B3
Northern Highland-American Legion SF - Plum Lake	20	B3
Northern Highland-American Legion SF - Razorback Lake	21	B3
Northern Highland-American Legion SF - Sandy Beach Lake	22	B3
Northern Highland-American Legion SF - South Trout Lake	23	B3
Northern Highland-American Legion SF - Starrett Lake	24	B3
Northern Highland-American Legion SF - Upper Gresham Lake	25	B3
Northern Highland-American Legion SF - West Star Lake	26	B3
Peshtigo River SF - Old Veterans Lake	29	C4
Point Beach SF	42	D4

1 • A1 | Brule River SF - Copper Range

Total sites: 15, RV sites: 15, Central water, Vault/pit toilet, No showers, No RV dump, Tent & RV camping: $21, Not plowed in winter, Stay limit: 14 days, Open all year, Reservations accepted, Elev: 997ft/304m, Tel: 715-372-5678, Nearest town: Brule. GPS: 46.609164, -91.579051

2 • A1 | Copper Range - Brule River SF

Total sites: 15, RV sites: 15, Central water, Vault/pit toilet, No showers, No RV dump, Tent & RV camping: $21, $5 off for WI residents, Daily entrance fee $11 ($8 WI residents), Lower off-season rates, Open all year, Elev: 997ft/304m, Tel: 715-372-5678, Nearest town: Brule. GPS: 46.610692, -91.579908

3 • B1 | Bois Brule - Brule River SF

Total sites: 20, RV sites: 17, Central water, Vault/pit toilet, No showers, No RV dump, Tent & RV camping: $21, $5 off for WI residents, Daily entrance fee $11 ($8 WI residents), Lower off-season rates, Stay limit: 14 days, Open all year, Elev: 978ft/298m, Tel: 715-372-5678, Nearest town: Brule. GPS: 46.538973, -91.592684

4 • B1 | Brule River SF - Bois Brule

Total sites: 20, RV sites: 17, Central water, Vault/pit toilet, No showers, No RV dump, Tent & RV camping: $21, Also walk-to sites, Not plowed in winter, 3, Stay limit: 14 days, Open all year, Reservations accepted, Elev: 978ft/298m, Tel: 715-372-5678, Nearest town: Brule. GPS: 46.541063, -91.591426

5 • B1 | Governor Knowles SF - St Croix

Total sites: 30, RV sites: 30, Central water, Vault/pit toilet, No showers, RV dump, Tent & RV camping: $21, $5 off for WI residents, Daily entrance fee $11 ($8 WI residents), Stay limit: 14 days, Open May-Oct, Reservations not accepted, Elev: 899ft/274m, Tel: 715-463-2898, Nearest town: Grantsburg. GPS: 45.764665, -92.778484

6 • B1 | Governor Knowles SF - Trade River Horse Camp

Total sites: 40, RV sites: 40, Central water, Vault/pit toilet, No showers, RV dump, Tent & RV camping: $21, $5 off for WI residents, Daily entrance fee $11 ($8 WI residents), Stay limit: 14 days, Open Apr-Nov, Reservations not accepted, Elev: 833ft/254m, Tel: 715-463-2898, Nearest town: Grantsburg. GPS: 45.598877, -92.773725

7 • B2 | Flambeau River SF - Connor Lake

Total sites: 29, RV sites: 29, Elec sites: 4, Central water, Vault/pit toilet, No showers, RV dump, Tents: $21/RVs: $31, $5 off for WI residents, Daily entrance fee $11 ($8 WI residents), Stay limit: 14 days, Open May-Sep, Reservations accepted, Elev: 1417ft/432m, Tel: 715-332-5271, Nearest town: Winter. GPS: 45.739979, -90.745718

8 • B2 | Flambeau River SF - Lake Of The Pines

Total sites: 30, RV sites: 30, Central water, Vault/pit toilet, No showers, No RV dump, Tent & RV camping: $21, $5 off for WI residents, Daily entrance fee $11 ($8 WI residents), Stay limit: 14 days, Open Apr-Nov, Reservations accepted, Elev: 1444ft/440m, Tel: 715-332-5271, Nearest town: Winter. GPS: 45.783318, -90.715446

9 • B3 | Northern Highland-American Legion SF - Big Lake

Total sites: 72, RV sites: 72, Central water, Vault/pit toilet, No showers, No RV dump, Tent & RV camping: $21, Not plowed in winter, $5 off for WI residents, Daily entrance fee $11 ($8 WI residents), Generator hours: 1000-1700, Open all year, Elev: 1660ft/506m, Tel: 715-356-3668, Nearest town: Woodruff. GPS: 46.164805, -89.788424

10 • B3 | Northern Highland-American Legion SF - Buffalo Lake

Total sites: 52, RV sites: 52, Central water, Vault/pit toilet, No showers, No RV dump, Tent & RV camping: $21, $5 off for WI residents, Daily entrance fee $11 ($8 WI residents), Generator hours: 1000-1700, Open May-Oct, Elev: 1650ft/503m, Tel: 715-356-3668, Nearest town: Woodruff. GPS: 45.876932, -89.563824

11 • B3 | Northern Highland-American Legion SF - Carrol Lake

Total sites: 19, RV sites: 12, Central water, Vault/pit toilet, No showers, No RV dump, Tent & RV camping: $21, Not plowed in winter, $5 off for WI residents, Daily entrance fee $11 ($8 WI residents), Generator hours: 1000-1700, Open all year, Elev: 1611ft/491m, Tel: 715-356-3668, Nearest town: Woodruff. GPS: 45.888507, -89.634637

12 • B3 | Northern Highland-American Legion SF - Clear Lake

Total sites: 101, RV sites: 90, Central water, Flush toilet, Free showers, RV dump, Tent & RV camping: $25, $5 off for WI residents, Daily entrance fee $11 ($8 WI residents), Generator hours: 1000-1700, Open all year, Elev: 1591ft/485m, Tel: 715-356-3668, Nearest town: Woodruff. GPS: 45.863889, -89.646019

13 • B3 | Northern Highland-American Legion SF - Crystal Lake

Total sites: 101, RV sites: 94, Central water, Flush toilet, Free showers, RV dump, Tent & RV camping: $25, Not plowed in winter, $5 off for WI residents, Daily entrance fee $11 ($8 WI residents), Generator hours: 1000-1700, Open all year, Elev: 1670ft/509m, Tel: 715-356-3668, Nearest town: Woodruff. GPS: 46.001411, -89.606821

14 • B3 | Northern Highland-American Legion SF - Cunard Lake

Total sites: 33, RV sites: 28, Central water, Vault/pit toilet, No showers, No RV dump, Tent & RV camping: $21, $5 off for WI residents, Daily entrance fee $11 ($8 WI residents), No generators, Open May-Sep, Elev: 1654ft/504m, Tel: 715-356-3668, Nearest town: Woodruff. GPS: 45.847156, -89.583413

15 • B3 | Northern Highland-American Legion SF - East Star Lake

Total sites: 30, RV sites: 30, Central water, Vault/pit toilet, No showers, No RV dump, Tent & RV camping: $21, $5 off for WI residents, Daily entrance fee $11 ($8 WI residents), Generator hours: 1000-1700, Open May-Nov, Reservations not accepted, Elev: 1713ft/522m, Tel: 715-356-3668, Nearest town: Woodruff. GPS: 46.025845, -89.465806

16 • B3 | Northern Highland-American Legion SF - Firefly Lake

Total sites: 71, RV sites: 71, Central water, Flush toilet, Free showers, No RV dump, Tent & RV camping: $25, Not plowed in winter, $5 off for WI residents, Daily entrance fee $11 ($8 WI residents), Generator hours: 1000-1700, Open all year, Elev: 1690ft/515m, Tel: 715-356-3668, Nearest town: Woodruff. GPS: 46.001667, -89.631816

17 • B3 | Northern Highland-American Legion SF - Indian Mounds

Total sites: 39, RV sites: 32, Central water, Vault/pit toilet, No showers, No RV dump, Tent & RV camping: $21, Not plowed in winter, $5 off for WI residents, Daily entrance fee $11 ($8 WI residents), Generator hours: 1000-1700, Open all year, Elev: 1611ft/491m, Tel: 715-356-3668, Nearest town: Woodruff. GPS: 45.824402, -89.638103

18 • B3 | Northern Highland-American Legion SF - Musky Lake

Total sites: 82, RV sites: 82, Central water, Flush toilet, Free showers, No RV dump, Tent & RV camping: $25, $5 off for WI residents, Daily entrance fee $11 ($8 WI residents), Generator hours: 1000-1700, Elev: 1693ft/516m, Tel: 715-356-3668, Nearest town: Woodruff. GPS: 46.006412, -89.611285

19 • B3 | Northern Highland-American Legion SF - North Trout Lake

Total sites: 48, RV sites: 48, Central water, Vault/pit toilet, No showers, RV dump, Tent & RV camping: $21, Not plowed in winter, $5 off for WI residents, Daily entrance fee $11 ($8 WI residents), Generator hours: 1000-1700, Open all year, Reservations not accepted, Elev: 1683ft/513m, Tel: 715-356-3668, Nearest town: Woodruff. GPS: 46.066768, -89.648258

20 • B3 | Northern Highland-American Legion SF - Plum Lake

Total sites: 18, RV sites: 16, Central water, Vault/pit toilet, No showers, No RV dump, Tent & RV camping: $21, $5 off for WI residents, Daily entrance fee $11 ($8 WI residents), Generator hours: 1000-1700, Open May-Sep, Elev: 1667ft/508m, Tel: 715-356-3668, Nearest town: Woodruff. GPS: 45.993116, -89.555456

21 • B3 | Northern Highland-American Legion SF - Razorback Lake

Total sites: 54, RV sites: 47, Central water, Vault/pit toilet, No showers, No RV dump, Tent & RV camping: $21, Not plowed in winter, $5 off for WI residents, Daily entrance fee $11 ($8 WI residents), Generator hours: 1000-1700, Open all year, Reservations not accepted, Elev: 1696ft/517m, Tel: 715-356-3668, Nearest town: Woodruff. GPS: 46.024992, -89.530759

22 • B3 | Northern Highland-American Legion SF - Sandy Beach Lake

Total sites: 33, RV sites: 30, Central water, Vault/pit toilet, No showers, No RV dump, Tent & RV camping: $21, $5 off for WI residents, Daily entrance fee $11 ($8 WI residents), Generator hours: 1000-1700, Open May-Nov, Elev: 1611ft/491m, Tel: 715-356-3668, Nearest town: Woodruff. GPS: 46.102633, -89.967451

23 • B3 | Northern Highland-American Legion SF - South Trout Lake

Total sites: 23, RV sites: 19, Central water, Vault/pit toilet, No showers, No RV dump, Tent & RV camping: $21, $5 off for WI residents, Daily entrance fee $11 ($8 WI residents), Generator hours: 1000-1700, Open May-Sep, Elev: 1650ft/503m, Tel: 715-356-3668, Nearest town: Woodruff. GPS: 46.021893, -89.654737

24 • B3 | Northern Highland-American Legion SF - Starrett Lake

Total sites: 44, RV sites: 38, Central water, Vault/pit toilet, No showers, No RV dump, Tent & RV camping: $21, $5 off for WI residents, Daily entrance fee $11 ($8 WI residents), No generators, Open May-Oct, Reservations not accepted, Elev: 1693ft/516m, Tel: 715-356-3668, Nearest town: Woodruff. GPS: 46.026745, -89.567475

25 • B3 | Northern Highland-American Legion SF - Upper Gresham Lake

Total sites: 26, RV sites: 23, Central water, Vault/pit toilet, No showers, No RV dump, Tent & RV camping: $21, $5 off for WI residents, Daily entrance fee $11 ($8 WI residents), Generator hours: 1000-1700, Open May-Oct, Reservations not accepted, Elev: 1647ft/502m, Tel: 715-356-3668, Nearest town: Woodruff. GPS: 46.075829, -89.728086

26 • B3 | Northern Highland-American Legion SF - West Star Lake

Total sites: 18, RV sites: 18, Central water, Vault/pit toilet, No showers, No RV dump, Tent & RV camping: $21, Not plowed in winter, $5 off for WI residents, Daily entrance fee $11 ($8 WI residents), Generator hours: 1000-1700, Open all year, Reservations not accepted, Elev: 1713ft/522m, Tel: 715-356-3668, Nearest town: Woodruff. GPS: 46.032199, -89.475035

27 • C2 | Black River SF - Castle Mound CG

Total sites: 35, RV sites: 35, Elec sites: 6, Central water, Flush toilet, Free showers, Tents: $23/RVs: $33, $5 off for WI residents, Daily entrance fee $11 ($8 WI residents), Lower off-season rates, Stay limit: 14 days, Open all year, Reservations accepted, Elev: 882ft/269m, Tel: 715-284-4103, Nearest town: Black River Falls. GPS: 44.282952, -90.828417

28 • C2 | Black River SF - East Fork CG

Total sites: 24, RV sites: 24, Central water, Vault/pit toilet, No showers, No RV dump, Tent & RV camping: $23, $5 off for WI residents, Daily entrance fee $11 ($8 WI residents), Lower off-season rates, Stay limit: 14 days, Open Apr-Nov, Reservations accepted, Elev: 928ft/283m, Tel: 715-284-4103, Nearest town: Hatfield. GPS: 44.417407, -90.675398

29 • C4 | Peshtigo River SF - Old Veterans Lake

Total sites: 15, RV sites: 15, Central water, Vault/pit toilet, Tent & RV camping: $21-23, $5 off for WI residents, Daily entrance fee $11 ($8 WI residents), Lower off-season rates, Stay limit: 14 days, Open Apr-Dec, Reservations accepted, Elev: 925ft/282m, Nearest town: Crivitz. GPS: 45.347828, -88.199356

30 • D2 | Black River SF - Pigeon Creek CG

Total sites: 38, RV sites: 38, Central water, No toilets, No showers, No RV dump, Tent & RV camping: $23, $5 off for WI residents, Daily entrance fee $11 ($8 WI residents), Lower off-season rates, Stay limit: 14 days, Open all year, Reservations accepted, Elev: 984ft/300m, Tel: 715-284-4103, Nearest town: Black River Falls. GPS: 44.213413, -90.618485

31 • D2 | Kickapoo Valley Reserve - Bare Beach - KRMB

Total sites: 1, No water, No toilets, Tent & RV camping: $15, No camping on beach, Reservations not accepted, Elev: 846ft/258m, Tel: 608-625-2960, Nearest town: LaFarge. GPS: 43.649454, -90.593068

32 • D2 | Kickapoo Valley Reserve - Bridge Seven - KRMB

Total sites: 1, No water, No toilets, Tent & RV camping: $15, Reservations not accepted, Elev: 839ft/256m, Tel: 608-625-2960, Nearest town: LaFarge. GPS: 43.672904, -90.595473

33 • D2 | Kickapoo Valley Reserve - Cutoff Camp

Total sites: 1, No water, No toilets, Tent & RV camping: $15, Reservations not accepted, Elev: 896ft/273m, Tel: 608-625-2960, Nearest town: LaFarge. GPS: 43.645157, -90.588077

34 • D2 | Kickapoo Valley Reserve - Daines Valley - KRMB

Total sites: 1, No water, No toilets, Tent & RV camping: $15, Reservations not accepted, Elev: 902ft/275m, Tel: 608-625-2960, Nearest town: LaFarge. GPS: 43.628313, -90.629785

35 • D2 | Kickapoo Valley Reserve - Hay Valley - KRMB

Total sites: 1, No water, No toilets, Tent & RV camping: $15, Access "tricky", Reservations not accepted, Elev: 912ft/278m, Tel: 608-625-2960, Nearest town: LaFarge. GPS: 43.678595, -90.607437

36 • D2 | Kickapoo Valley Reserve - Jug Creek

Total sites: 1, No water, No toilets, Tent & RV camping: $15, Reservations not accepted, Elev: 850ft/259m, Tel: 608-625-2960, Nearest town: LaFarge. GPS: 43.626537, -90.592375

37 • D2 | Kickapoo Valley Reserve - Mule Camp - KRMB

Total sites: 1, No water, No toilets, Tent & RV camping: $15, Reservations not accepted, Elev: 938ft/286m, Tel: 608-625-2960, Nearest town: LaFarge. GPS: 43.620826, -90.613001

38 • D2 | Kickapoo Valley Reserve - Potts Corners - KRMB

Total sites: 1, No water, No toilets, Tent & RV camping: $15, Reservations not accepted, Elev: 837ft/255m, Tel: 608-625-2960, Nearest town: LaFarge. GPS: 43.630322, -90.650039

39 • D4 | Kettle Moraine SF - Pike Lake Unit

Total sites: 32, RV sites: 32, Elec sites: 11, Central water, Flush toilet, Free showers, RV dump, Tents: $23-25/RVs: $33-35, $5 off for WI residents, Daily entrance fee $11 ($8 WI residents), Lower off-season rates, Open Apr-Oct, Reservations accepted, Elev: 1217ft/371m, Tel: 262-670-3400, Nearest town: Hartford. GPS: 43.315836, -88.306445

40 • D4 | Long Lake - Kettle-Moraine SF

Total sites: 200, RV sites: 200, Central water, Flush toilet, Free showers, RV dump, Tent & RV camping: $23-25, Stay limit: 14 days, Open May-Sep, Elev: 1056ft/322m, Tel: 920-533-8612, Nearest town: Campbellsport. GPS: 43.663735, -88.165329

41 • D4 | Mauthe Lake - Kettle-Moraine SF

Total sites: 135, RV sites: 135, Elec sites: 51, Central water, Flush toilet, Free showers, RV dump, Tents: $23-25/RVs: $33-35, Stay limit: 14 days, Open all year, Elev: 1007ft/307m, Tel: 262-626-2116, Nearest town: Beechwood. GPS: 43.603868, -88.173995

42 • D4 | Point Beach SF

Total sites: 127, RV sites: 127, Elec sites: 70, Central water, Flush toilet, Free showers, RV dump, Tents: $25-27/RVs: $35-37, $5 off for WI residents, Daily entrance fee $11 ($8 WI residents), Lower off-season rates, Stay limit: 14 days, Open all year, Reservations accepted, Elev: 607ft/185m, Tel: 920-794-7480, Nearest town: Two Rivers. GPS: 44.213451, -87.509575

43 • E3 | Kettle-Moraine SF - Horseriders

Total sites: 56, RV sites: 56, Elec sites: 19, Central water, Flush toilet, Free showers, No RV dump, Tents: $23-25/RVs: $33-35, Must have horse, $5 off for WI residents, Daily entrance fee $11 ($8 WI residents), Lower off-season rates, Stay limit: 14 days, Open Apr-Nov, Elev: 879ft/268m, Tel: 262-594-6200, Nearest town: Palmyra. GPS: 42.868478, -88.577081

44 • E3 | Kettle-Moraine SF - Whitewater

Total sites: 63, RV sites: 63, Central water, Vault/pit toilet, No showers, RV dump, Tent & RV camping: $23-25, $5 off for WI residents, Daily entrance fee $11 ($8 WI residents), Lower off-season rates, Stay limit: 14 days, Open May-Oct, Reservations accepted, Elev: 945ft/288m, Tel: 262-473-7501, Nearest town: Whitewater. GPS: 42.784254, -88.694821

45 • E4 | Kettle-Moraine SF - Ottawa Lake

Total sites: 100, RV sites: 100, Elec sites: 49, Central water, Flush toilet, Free showers, RV dump, Tents: $23-25/RVs: $33-35, $5 off for WI residents, Daily entrance fee $11 ($8 WI residents), Lower off-season rates, Stay limit: 14 days, Open all year, Reservations accepted, Elev: 889ft/271m, Tel: 262-594-6220, Nearest town: Ottawa. GPS: 42.937871, -88.474772

46 • E4 | Kettle-Moraine SF - Pinewoods

Total sites: 101, RV sites: 101, Central water, Flush toilet, Free showers, RV dump, Tent & RV camping: $23-25, $5 off for WI residents, Daily entrance fee $11 ($8 WI residents), Lower off-season rates, Stay limit: 14 days, Open May-Oct, Reservations accepted, Elev: 1050ft/320m, Tel: 262-594-6220, Nearest town: Ottawa. GPS: 42.961188, -88.443941